Laugh out Loud!
Kids
By Sharon Irish

Laugh out Loud! Kids
Copyright: Sharon Irish
ISBN: 978-0-9926375-8-3
Published: 4th January 2015
Publisher: Sharon Irish
Cover by: Sharon Irish

The right of Sharon Irish to be identified as author of this Work has been asserted by her in accordance with sections 77 and 78 of the Copyright, Designs and Patents Act 1988.
All rights reserved. No part of this publication may be reproduced, stored in retrieval system, copied in any form or by any means, electronic, mechanical, photocopying, recording or otherwise transmitted without written permission from the publisher. You must not circulate this book in any format.

Firstly, a little bit about this book:-

At the time of writing, I have a three year old little boy and a five month old little girl. My little boy reminds me daily of the reason I wanted to create this book, he is frequently making me laugh with the things he says and does. His understanding of the world around him is growing daily thanks to all the questions he asks (constantly!) His questions can be funny, cheeky or downright embarrassing depending on the situation we are in when he asks, and as my other Mum friends will agree, every child has their Parents in fits of giggles, pulling their hair out or hiding away in horror with their comments (which are usually said in the loudest voice possible).

Our Three year old is now toilet trained which actually wasn't as bad an experience as I thought it would be however we now have to be prepared for him saying (or shouting) "I want a wee" when we are in the car or at the till in the supermarket, when he has to go, he really has to go!

I love reading other people's stories but this collection has been by far my favourite – it has been quite hard to put together as I have spent half my time laughing and not able to fully concentrate!

I really hope you enjoy reading this book, and these stories give you something to giggle at, maybe even laugh out loud!

Sharon Irish

Laugh Out Loud!
Kids

Mixing Up Words and Misunderstandings:-..............8

Copying:-...26

Embarrassing Comments and Actions:-...................30

Kids Know Best:-………………………………………………….52

Telling Tales and Getting Parents In Trouble:-……..62

Cheeky But Funny Comments and Attitude:-..........66

Observations and Understanding of a Child:-………76

Cute and Random Comments and Actions:-………104

Inquisitive Kids and Questions:-…………………………124

Honesty:-……………………………………………………………..134

Dishonesty and Deviousness:-……………………………144

Kids' Comments on A New Baby On The Way (Taken From My First Book Laugh Out Loud Pregnancy!):………………………………………………………..148

Kids' Comments on New Baby When Here (Taken From My Second Book Laugh Out Loud Babies!):.174

Mixing Up Words and Misunderstandings:-

One word can mean many things and different words can mean the same thing, some words sound the same but mean completely different things – this is confusing enough for adults, never mind children!

My eighteen month old had a stomach bug and was crying a lot. My seven year old said "She is crying her balls out Mum!"
I said "Don't you mean bawling her eyes out?"
I couldn't help but burst out laughing!
Kerri, UK

My Daughter says "See you tomato" instead of "See you tomorrow."
Emma, UK

My Son was telling me the other day "Granddad has got a new 'mumbawower' Mummy." Meaning he has a new

'lawnmower' Ha Ha!
Lorraine, UK

When my Daughter was two and had her first day at Nursery, our conversation went like this:-

Me: "Did you have a nice day?"
Her: "Yes Mummy."
Me: "What did you have for lunch?"
Her: "Properly."
Me: "Do you mean broccoli?"
Her: "No, properly, the Teacher said I was eating properly."
Rhona, UK

My Little girl came home from school one day and told me "I am absolutely sausaged."
It took me hours to figure out she was trying to say 'exhausted.' Ha Ha!
Lesley, UK

My best friend was over with his little boy, a toddler at the time. The little boy was running around my room and then decided to remove his socks. I asked him to take them to Daddy so he could put them back on. He walked up to the dog and lifted his foot up, holding out the socks. He almost got it, 'doggy', 'Daddy', So close!
Kelsey, USA

I was at the Doctor's surgery today waiting for my little boy to have his immunisation and he went to a toy kitchen where these girls about two and a half or three years old were playing. My little boy started to try to 'break in' to the till and one of the girls said "Stop! Leave the till I'm going to call the ambulance to arrest you!" This made my day, I was laughing so much!
Ruth, UK

When my Son was in Nursery he took great pleasure in informing me and my Husband that he had been learning about snails and their 'testicles.' It was hard to keep a straight face while he was explaining!
Joanne, UK

Apparently when I was little I was trying to say something and it wouldn't come out so my mum said to me ''Just spit it out'' so I stopped talking and spat on the floor! I don't remember doing this but she insists on telling everyone about it.
Kirsty, UK

When I was younger, my Mum was trying to explain the difference between cucumbers and courgettes and I said "Doesn't Sue next door smoke courettes?"
Shirley, UK

These are some funny examples of my girls mixing words up:
"Mum should I put my coat on the radigator?" (Coat on

the radiator)
"Mummy did you know that the rhinosopus is maffise?"
(Rhinoceros is massive)
"Wow its really froggy out there." (Foggy)
"Can we go to double-oh on holiday?" (Can we go to Dublin)
Jenny, UK

When my Son was three and a half and was going to Pre-school, he was asking the Teacher if he could borrow something from her. The teacher asked him "what are the magic words?"
He thought for a few seconds and said, "Abra-cadabra?"
Helen, UK

My Son always makes me laugh, the other day he was doing head stands on my sofa (a big no-no) and said "Mummy, look at me I'm doing an ass stand!" I couldn't tell him off because I was laughing so much!
Rachel, UK

This morning over breakfast I asked my Son "Are you looking forward to going to Nursery?" He replied by slapping his head and saying "Mummy I can't look backwards, I'd crash into things, aren't you silly Mummy?" I tried to explain what I meant but that seemed to make him more confused!
Laura, UK

We were eating one day and I was watching my Son (who likes his food!) I said to my Husband "I wish I could be like him, he eats like a horse and never gains an ounce of fat." My boy then proceeded to drop his knife and fork and put his face in his food to eat (like a horse!) I keep forgetting how literally children think!
Karla, UK

My Daughter who was three was reading a book and shouted "Look! A nipple! A nipple!" She was pointing at her book so I looked down at it and saw a hippo!
Charlotte, UK

I was serving my Son his dinner and I said "I hope you like your pizza, Mummy made it from scratch." My Son looked back at me in horror and asked "Who's Scratch?" I tried to explain whilst trying not to giggle Ha Ha!
Nicola, UK

We were out shopping the other day and my two year old asked "Can we go up the alligator?" He meant the 'escalator'!
Sammy, UK

When on holiday recently we regularly went to a restaurant near our apartment. The Head Waiter always greeted us with "Hola!" (As they do in Spain!) After a few days, my little girl said, "I want to go see 'Hola' in the cafe please."

Bless her, she thought his name was Hola!
Madeline, UK

My Daughter calls the computer the 'pooter,' her scooter her 'cooter,' her sunglasses are her 'sunglarglars' and a caterpillar is a 'caterpeepee.' Her favourite toys in bed are her pink 'neigh neigh' (you can all guess what that is!). She calls Mary Poppins 'Mary Popov!'
She also asks to watch 'two nuns' (the Sound of Music!), and when she is tired or it's dark she says "It's bednight."
Caroline, UK

My Son said the other day "Quick, look! There is a robber in the garden!" (Robin)
Claire, Southborough, UK

My Daughter is a preschooler now, but her pronunciation of things makes me laugh all the time. Examples are "Where are my aliens?" (Sylvanian Family figures), and when she sings the months of the year song, she always says "Remember" instead of November!
Diane, UK

My youngest asked "Mum, why do we call this 'Dalek' bread, do Dalek's eat it?"
I said, "Err, no sweetie, it's called garlic bread!"
Fiona, UK

My Daughter who is five came running downstairs one day and said "Mummy I think I have a coleslaw." I think she meant a 'cold sore!'
Cheryl, UK

When our Daughter was about three we went on holiday. She had habit of putting an 'e' on the end of her animals e.g. 'dogee,' 'catee,' 'birdee' etc. I had patiently explained that animals don't have e's, they are dogs, cats, birds etc. We were on the beach later and she said "Mommy can I go on the donk?"
I wasn't sure how to get out of that one!
Kaitlyn, USA

I was talking to my Husband about names for our new baby with my Son present, and mentioned Victoria Beckham's little girl, 'Harper Seven'. My Son gave me a really puzzled look and said "Why would you call your kid 'half past seven'?"
Georgina, UK

My Brother and his Partner (same sex) are thinking of adopting, we were discussing it last week and explaining to my 5 year old Nephew that the baby would have two Daddies. My seven year old Niece then piped up with "My friend has two Mummies, they're Columbians!" She meant lesbians of course!
Jennifer, UK

Laugh Out Loud! Kids

My little girl who is five soon made me laugh today. She asked "Mama, please may I borrow the iPad?"
"Why?" I asked her.
"Because I'd like to send a 'me-mail' to myself using the 'internext.'"
I Love that girl.
Jordan, USA

My Daughter said this morning, "I'm feeling a bit 'sneezable' today."
Emily, UK

In the car, a few months back, the kids (five and six) decided to play their own version of 'I spy.' They were 'spying' animals and my Daughter said to her six year old Brother "I spy with my little eye, an animal beginning with L."
"Elephant!" was his reply!
Natalie, UK

I wanted my five year old Son to clean his room so I said to him "Go and make your room all clean and sparkly." Ten minutes later I went to check on him and he had thrown glitter over his entire room! His response to my gasp of horror was "But Mummy, you told me to make it sparkly!" I should have been more careful with what I said!
Vicky, UK

When my Daughter was about two and a half I was hanging out the washing when she exclaimed "Mummy, I can see your booby-knickers!" Meaning my bra! Ha Ha! I nicely asked her not to say that, and that it was called a bra.
Charly, UK

We were on a plane a few years ago and had some Fruit pastilles (sweets). My Granny gave one to my Son, saying it was for his ears, so he took her at her word and stuck it in his ear!
Laurie, UK

My Daughter was about three and came running in from the garden saying "Mummy, mummy! I found an intersex!" It was a ladybird and she meant 'insect'!
Maria, UK

A few weeks ago our car was in the garage for some repairs. After my Husband left to pick it up, my Daughter asked where he'd gone. I told her "Daddy's gone to pick the car up." An hour later when my Husband got home my Daughter announced "Oh Daddy's put the car down now!"
Amy, UK

This is so embarrassing, but hopefully funny for those reading it:
I was picking my Daughter up one day when she said to her Pre-school Teacher "My Daddy was playing with his

c**k at the weekend cos mummy fiddled too much and broke it."
I honestly could have died at that moment - the Clock had stopped working so I tried to replace the battery but somehow snapped a spring off in the process and so my Husband told me I always fiddle with his things too much! I explained this to the teacher but left red as a grape!
Donna, UK

We were due to go to a family funeral and my Son kindly informed me that they would be 'planting' Auntie in the ground during her burial!
Kelly, UK

My Daughter said (sniffing her underarm) "Eww! Armpit breath!" And then on another occasion said "'I've got crumbs in my socks." (pins and needles)
Michelle, UK

My Son used to call coke 'beer' when he was small and when we were in Tesco once he said "Mum can I have some beer?" My mum (knowing he meant coke) said "Yes I'll get it when I get to that aisle" as an elderly lady looked on in horror!
Mia, UK

My two year old just discovered 'Jammy Dodgers'. The only thing is he keeps calling them "Daddy's Stodgers!"
Rebecca, UK

I shout "enough" at my dogs when they bark, to keep them quiet. My toddler however tries to copy me but shouts "muff!" Rather embarrassing when out walking them in the park!
Carol, UK

My Daughter was watching 'Elmo' on TV one day and made me laugh when she said "Look Mummy, its Elbow!'
Michaela, UK

When I was about five, I came out of School at home time after doing P.E. and my Mum looked at me and said "Your shoes are on the wrong feet" so I looked back with a confused expression and said "Who's feet should they be on?"
Emily, UK

My two year old loved 'Thomas the Tank Engine' but had a bit of trouble getting his tongue around the 'Fat Controller'. I will never forget the first time he pointed at the TV and yelled "Mummy it's the f***ing roller!"
When he was five years old he got into 'Star Wars' and used to call 'Darth Vader' the "Dark Favour" which had us in stiches.
Mel, UK

When my Husband asked our two year old if she was

Mexican she said "No! I'm a good girl!"
Clare, USA

My two year old in a toy shop - "Ooh I want to have this! I think I will ask Uncle Christmas!"
Jennifer, UK

My Daughter when she was two was looking at old picture of my Mom and Dad before they had kids. My Mom was telling her "That's Grandma and Grandpa a long time ago," pointing at the picture. My Daughter asked her "How did you get the picture, Grandma?" My Mom said "Someone took the picture of us" and my Daughter said "Well it's lucky you got it back!"
We were in stitches at her logic!
Shelley, USA

My 3 year old came home from 'Disney on Ice' with a Mickey Mouse hat, and when she put it on she said, "But Mom I want to be Mickey Mouse, but I don't have a tail, maybe we could get one at the tail store!" I thought that was priceless.
Cora, USA

My Son who was three at the time was helping his Grandpa with the yard work. Grandpa asked Nathan if he wanted to go fishing when they were done with their work, Nathan very seriously nods his head and says "Yes! Ya know, Grandpa, I haven't been fishing in years!"
Crystal, USA

I was shopping with my six year old Daughter, looking through the clothes racks (in my size). She grabbed a shirt off the rack and said "Mommy, this one's really cute, now all I have to do is buy some boobs."
I just about fell over! I then realized she meant a bra!
Aimee, USA

Just recently my Son who is eight years old has been calling his new Sister's umbilical cord her "extension cord." Ha Ha!
Tanya, UK

My 4 year old Son didn't realise I was in his room and when he saw me he shouted "You scared the life out of my skin!"
Paula, UK

My little girl asked me the other day "Can I put my willie boots on so I can jump in the cuddles?" So cute!
Deborah, UK

I am Italian and my Husband is a farmer. So we eat spaghetti a lot and are always around tractors! I thought I was going to die laughing when to my surprise my Son asked me to "Pass the Farmer John Cheese" (parmesan cheese) the other night at dinner!
Toni, USA

Laugh Out Loud! Kids

We were out shopping and were just pulling into our last stop when my Daughter noticed we were stopping and asked if she was going in too (since it was just me in the car with her and her baby sister, this was a bit of a no-brainer!). I said "Yes" and she held up her feet and showed me she had just removed her shoes (again). I told her, "Mommy doesn't like it when you take your shoes off like that." Her response? "If you don't like it you can get your money back!"
Dawn, USA

On the way home from picking up the kids, my Daughter announced that she wanted a grilled cheese sandwich for dinner. We decided to stop and pick up something at the drive through. I told my Husband to order her (our three year old) a grilled cheese and get one for our Son (five year old) too. The three year old said "He not want a girl cheese samich Mommy, he want a boy cheese samich!" She'll never live that one down!
Amy, USA

My little Brother started crying in his car seat on a trip to our holiday home. It was a hot day and my Dad had just stopped to get us all a cold pop to drink. My Mum and Dad, very concerned, asked him what the matter was. He said "Daddy, you're not supposed to drink and drive!" It still makes me giggle after all these years!
Lisa, UK

My three year old was going potty while my Husband was in the shower. My Husband finished and got out while my Daughter was still going. Seeing him naked she asked, "Daddy is that your tail?" referring to his, well you know. He said "No it's my penis." She replied, "Your peanut?" I never laughed so hard, my Husband didn't think it was quite as funny!

Oh I have so many! One of my favorites was when I couldn't help my older Son because I was nursing my baby, and my oldest looked at me and said, "Don't worry Mommy, I've got it under the troll." Oh I laughed so hard!
Anna, USA

I was trying to potty train my Son when he was two. I left his diaper off and told him if he put his poop in the potty, I'd give him a cookie. I saw him run past me and he was holding poop! I screamed, "No!" But he did what he always did when he had something he wasn't supposed to have and got caught - he threw it at me! Luckily I was able to get out of the way, but I couldn't console him until I assured him he could still have a cookie once the mess was cleaned up. Ugh!
Melanie, USA

My Daughter was coloring in a notebook while lying on the floor. I asked her to color on the table. She whimpered for a while about not wanting to, until finally she stood up, walked to the table and colored on actual table. I asked her what she was doing and she said, "What you told me, are you crazy?"
Jen, USA

I asked my Son (who was just in his underwear) to put on "some other clothes" and he said "I don't wear Mother clothes! I'm a kid, I wear kid clothes!"
Freya, USA

My two year old says 'Superman' as "Pooperman" So he runs around the house yelling "I Pooperman!" Which sometimes is totally appropriate!
Janice, USA

My Son was putting a cap back on the marker he was using. He started turning and turning to get it on. Then with utter concentration he proclaimed, "I is busy screwing." How could I not chuckle? I hope he doesn't say that out loud in public!
Lori, USA

When my Son was about to turn three we asked him what he wanted for his Birthday. My Husband is a truck driver, so we weren't surprised when he said "A CB radio." We were in complete shock when he said "With a hooker". It took us a little bit to realize he was talking about a hook to hang the CB microphone on. Then, a couple days later, after my Husband mounted a CB on the bunk bed for him and my Son was asking daily for a hooker, he finally found an old one and brought it up along with a screw driver to attach it to the bed. My Son looked at him so innocently and said "Daddy, are you going to screw my hooker?"
Nariah, USA

I can remember telling my Dad and Step Mum that my Mum had gone to be "seduced" when she was going to be 'Induced' with my little Brother!
Kelly, UK

One Christmas, while my Son was tearing the wrapping off his presents, I said to him, "Slow down a bit, I need to read the tags and see who they are from." and he said " Duh Mum!, Its off Farmer Christmas, you made me leave cookies for him last night, remember!"
Stacey, UK

When I put my Daughter to bed she will always ask me not to turn the dark on!
Millie, UK

Instead of saying, "One Mississippi", my Son says, "One Mr Chippy, two Mr Chippy."
He also says, "1,2,3 F*** off"! He's actually saying "Blast off" but it really doesn't sound like it. I have to say every time, "Yeah, blast off!"
Cheryl, UK

We drove by a house that was being built and was just being framed. My Daughter commented, "Oooh, I wouldn't want to live in a naked house like that!"
Lauren, UK

Laugh Out Loud! Kids

My phone 'died', as I put it. So I plugged it in to charge it and then went to run some errands. When I got back, my phone was nowhere to be seen. Turns out my Son had buried my 'dead' 200 dollar Blackberry because he felt sorry for me. Laugh or cry?
Terri, USA

My Son is 8 years old and he said something to his friends which I didn't hear. All the other kids were saying things like "I want to be a Fireman", and "I want to be a Cop". My son said "I want to get rich on the internet, I want to be an ant on the floor." We all started laughing, cause we knew that he meant 'Entrepreneur.'
Jodie, USA

I have lots of stories but my most cringe worthy one was when my Daughter (who was two at the time) had a bath with some 'Playmobile' Men and filled a cup with water and put the 'toy Men' in it. She asked loudly "Mummy would you like some Man juice?" It was funny, but I thought if any neighbours overheard (we had the window open), they may wonder what we were up to!
Cathy, UK

Copying:-

Our kids love to copy us, it helps them learn, but sometimes they copy things we thought they hadn't seen or heard. It can be hilarious watching your little 'mini-me' copying you, or it can be highly embarrassing, depending on the situation!

My Son is obsessed with saying "It's foggy." He'll say "Oh it's so foggy I can't see, we'll have to turn back, it's too dangerous!" I think he's been watching too much Fireman Sam!
Kerry, UK

When my Son goes to the bathroom to use the toilet, and I accidently walk in, he says "Excuse me, do you mind? Don't be so rudey Mummy!" Of course it's different when he wants to come in when *I'm* using the toilet!
Julia, UK

One day my Hubby was disciplining our Son and put him in the naughty corner, so he stood in the corner and shouted "Daddy, Daddy! Daddy! Am I speaking Chinese?" Oh my word, I could not move for laughing and needless to say, he didn't stay in the corner for the full two minutes!
Gemma, UK

My Daughter has started waddling when we are out courtesy of my Husband teaching her "This is how Mummy walks!" Thanks!
Patricia, UK

On my Mum's Birthday, as my Daughter gave her her present, my almost two year old told her "I bought that. Got a receipt." Cheeky monkey!
Leanne, UK

We were waiting at a crossing on our way to do some shopping and my eldest told a Man off for crossing before the Green Man came on (I'm teaching both boys the Green Cross Code). He was waggling his finger and looked very cross with the Man. I was proud but I did have a little chuckle.
Alison, UK

Our little boy has just learned to say "Hiya" and often puts phones to his ear and says it or remote controls. Today during dinner he slapped his homemade pizza slice on his

ear and said "Hiya!" It was so funny!
Amy, UK

My Son was messing around in front of the mirror and accidentally banged his head. He jumped up looked at himself in the mirror and asked "Is you okay?"
Mary, UK

I was at the Doctor's office last week for my Daughter's six month check-up. There were about five other people in the waiting room and it was really quiet. That was when my three year old Son said "Mommy I don't have time for this!" I guess he's been listening when I talk because I say that all the time!
Jenna, USA

About a month ago I woke to find my Son (he'll be 3 next month) standing at the foot of my bed wearing my blue fuzzy robe and my wedding shoes (3 inch heels). I'm a big picture taker but that was one of those moments where I was too busy laughing my ass off and waking my Husband to worry about the camera. The pics are in my head! He did get into the shoes again later that day and I got pics of it that time!
Leila, USA

On the morning of Kindergarten registration I offered to get coffee for the girls in the office. My Son and I took the orders and set off to the coffee shop. After returning and handing out the coffee to each one, including a Hot

Chocolate for my Son, it was his turn for his Kinder interview and test. After hearing his name called, he picked up his cup and started to walk into the room (no parents beyond the door). I offered to hold his drink for him but he replied "I'll need my coffee in my meeting Mommy!" Needless to say the entire office broke into laughter and after some fast talking he left his cup with me, went to his "meeting" and is now enjoying his Kindergarten year!
Sasha, USA

One morning, when my friend's Son was just three, he was going to the toilet whilst his Mum was getting dressed. He came out of the bathroom walking funny. When his Mum asked what the matter was, he said that he had stuck one of her plasters on and it really hurt. Whilst she peeled a firmly stuck sanitary towel away from his bottom and his bits, scarcely able to contain her laughter, his expression was dead pan when he asked if it hurt her when she used them!
Sarah, UK

Embarrassing Comments and Actions:-

I'm sure all the other Mums reading this will agree that Kids can be so embarrassing – they just say whatever is on their minds, just blurt it out with no thought as to how it may sound. If they see something they need to ask about, they will ask right then and there, even if we would prefer them not to!

I was at the check-out in the supermarket the other day with my Son (almost three) and I told him to hand his toy to the lady to pay to which he said (very loud and clear) "That's not a Lady, that's a Man!" She didn't say anything, just gave me a look - I couldn't wait to get out of there!
Maddie, UK

My Daughter pulled out a sanitary pad from my bag at her toddler group and was strutting about waving it around telling everyone it was Mummy's 'nappy!' It was a good job we were only around other Mums who totally understood!
Sam, UK

My Daughter is at the 'following me to the loo' stage. We were at my Father In Law's a couple of weeks ago and I went to the loo. My Daughter noticed me going and said "Wee wee" indicating that she needed to go so I said to her "Come on then." She came in with me the whole time saying "Mummy wee wee." I did what I had to do, I flushed the loo and whilst washing my hands my Daughter was standing at the toilet waving whilst saying "Bye wee wee". We came out of the toilet and went back into my Father In Law's kitchen and my Daughter ran off. She then came running back to me, lifted up my top, pointed at my lady area and said (in full view of everyone) "Mummy's wee wee gone now." I was very glad I had only gone for a wee or it could have been much more embarrassing!
Tina, UK

My three year old and I were in a supermarket and there was a member of staff (quite a large lady) carrying some boxes. My Daughter was wandering around and got in her way, so I told her to move out the way and look where she was going, to which she replied "Mum it wasn't my fault, that big fat lady got in *my* way!" I'm sure the Woman must have heard her and I was so embarrassed I had to walk out of the shop and tell my Daughter not to be so rude!
Stacey, UK

When he was about two or three, I had my Son sitting in the cart at the grocery store as I was shopping in the

produce section. In walks an old Woman with a cane, an eye patch and a cloth hair covering. My Son started bouncing up and down, pointing and screaming "Mommy! Mommy Look, a Pirate!" I couldn't even look at the Woman, everyone in the area turned to look at us. I was so red faced!
Lorna, USA

The following conversation took place in a supermarket, in the loudest voice that my three year old Niece can muster:

Niece: "There was poo in your house wasn't there Aunty?"
Me: "Yes sweetie, there was."
Niece: "I trod in it didn't I Aunty?"
Me: "Yes, you did."
Niece: "It wasn't very nice, was it Aunty?"
Me: "No honey, it wasn't."
Niece: "'Cause people don't normally have poo in their houses do they Aunty?"
Me: "No sweetie, they don't!"

I could have died from embarrassment!
Samantha, UK

I was reading a book about animal noises with my Son yesterday. We got to the rooster and I said "Cock-a-doodle dooooooo" to which he replied "Cock-n-loooo-n-loooooo." He then decided all the "n-looo-n-loooo" was too much bother so just went round for the next ten minutes saying "Cock cock cock cock cock cock".

I guess he liked how it sounded. Oops!
Katie, UK

My least favourite moments with my Kids are the ones when they point or stare at someone, as they tend to blurt right out what they see, for example when out shopping, hearing "Mummy, Mummy! Look how fat that Lady is!" When the Lady in question is in earshot is really embarrassing!
Kathryn, UK

I don't have any children yet but my friend brought her four year old Son to church, and he was squirming and making a lot of noise, so she picked him up. This made him squirm even more, so the more he squirmed, the tighter she squeezed him. This went on until she was squeezing him pretty tightly, and finally he screamed (in church!) "You're squeezing my pecker!" She dropped him quite quickly!
Toni, UK

When our Daughter came out of Nursery one day, she was grinning from ear to ear. My Husband asked her "Did you have a good day?" She replied "Yes thank you, nice to see you Daddy!" (He usually worked throughout the week but he got off early that day). He was really pleased but then the Teacher called us over and said "She has been very good today."
"Great" we said.
The Teacher then touched our Daughter's hair and asked "Where did you get this gorgeous red hair from?"

She replied "Its ginger, from my Daddy's ginger willy."
I laughed for ages, the teacher blushed a bright red, and my Husband didn't know whether to laugh or cry! In the end, he just turned a funny kind of red but remained speechless!
On the way home, my Husband said to our Daughter "Why did you say that to your Teacher? That was embarrassing!"
Our Daughter looked at him so innocently and said "Well, I was taught to always tell the truth, and no one else is ginger!"
He couldn't argue, she was right!
Leah, UK

I was walking with my Son one day on our way to the shops when I noticed some builders working on a house a little further up the road. My Son also noticed them and we had to walk past. He was staring all the way up to them when he blurted out, in his cute and innocent way (but also at the top of his voice), "Mummy why is that Man showing his bum?" I hurried him along, not looking back whilst the builders erupted in laughter!
Amanda, UK

My Mum told me the story of my older Brother when he was about two years old when we were all in a cafe, I was there too but I was only a few months old so I don't remember. Out loud my Brother asked "Daddy, why was you going err err err with Mummy in your bedroom?" My mum said the whole cafe went quiet and she couldn't wait to get out of there – they didn't remember what

they said to answer my Brother, but it obviously wasn't the truth!
Tina, UK

One summer my Sister put her bikini on and lay down in the garden to catch a few rays. Not long after, my two year old Nephew wandered over to her and asked "Mummy, where's your boobies gone?" I felt so bad for her, although I did laugh - her son is obviously about as tactful as his Father! Ha Ha!
Sharon, UK

My friend and her Nephew took the bus to my house one day and the Nephew pointed to a larger lady on the bus and said (loudly) "You're huge!" My Sister was mortified!
Ellen, USA

My friend recently told me something her five year old Daughter said to her. They were doing their supermarket shopping and got to the bathroom/hygiene section (which was rather busy) and as they walked past the tampons her daughter said to her "look Mum, there's those things you stick up your bum!" Nice and loud of course!
Oh the things I've got to look forward to when I have my own children!
Kaz, UK

I think my 5 year old Son is already a boob Man. When he was two and a half years old we were all 'trick-or-treating' for Halloween. My Daughter and I were a little ahead of

my Boyfriend and my Son, who were starting to come down the steps of a house after getting candy. My Son said something that my Boyfriend thought he said but had asked him repeat it. My Son then then repeated in a louder voice "She has big boobies!" The lady was still standing at her door. My Boyfriend was horrified and asked him not to say that as it was rude!"
Mandy, UK

I woke up one morning and went to the toilet and as usual, my three year old Son tagged along. I had started my period in the night and my Son noticed and asked, while chuckling away, "Mummy, why have you got jam in your pants?" I laughed and said "Erm, I'm not sure." I knew it would come up again and it did, but in front of the whole of my Partner's family later that day! I was horrified when he casually told everyone that Mummy had put jam in her pants that morning! I still cringe about it now! Horrible!
Gemma, UK

A few weeks ago there were people selling door to door in my area. They knocked on my door and while I was talking to them, my eldest came waddling up to me with his underpants round his ankles, potty in hand saying "Mummy! Mummy! I done a really big wee wee!"
That got rid of them pretty quickly!
Becky, UK

When I was about two or three I was on the bus with my Mum talking to some ladies. They were getting off before

us and we were near the back. When they got to the door I stood up and shouted "Bye bye old biddies!" (My Mum's Brothers called every one old biddies so I must have been copying!) My mum just wanted a hole to appear and swallow her!
Shannon, UK

Before she found out I was pregnant, I was in the middle of Argos with my Daughter when she said really loudly "Mummy you are so greedy! Look at your belly! You shouldn't eat McDonalds anymore!"
Karen, UK

We were out shopping and were at the checkout in one of the shops when my lovely Daughter asked the teenaged sales clerk serving us "Have you got chicken pox on your face?"
Aimee, UK

I was in Asda and stopped in the baby aisle to get my baby Daughter some dummies. There was a Woman already there, crouched down, looking for dummies too. When I stopped I noticed a funny smell and thought my baby may need changing. The Woman's little boy, he must have been about three years old, was stood holding onto her trolley and very proudly said to me "My Mummy made that smell."
I had to turn away because as much as I tried, I couldn't stop laughing. The poor Woman was beetroot red. I had to walk away and go back for the dummies later. As I was

walking away he was saying to her "Its ok Mummy, everybody does it."
Charlotte, UK

Years ago when I was a rep for a naughty lingerie Company I needed sweet shoe laces and chocolate for the games we used to play at the parties. When I went shopping I took my Daughter with me. When we got to the till, the cashier made a comment about the sweets we had. My darling Daughter then told her "We don't eat them, Mummy puts them in her knickers." I had to explain quickly and then run!
Claudia, UK

When I was walking into Nursery with my Son one day, a Man passed us who was a little on the large side. My three year old Son said (at the top of his voice) "look Mummy! That Man is a bit like Humpty Dumpty!" I didn't say anything, just carried on!
Jess, UK

My Daughter was three and we were sat on the bus when she started chatting to the Men sat behind us. She then looked at me and asked "Mummy I know that's a Man, but what is that other one?" Thankfully he and his friend found the funny side, while I cringed!
Hannah, UK

Whilst queuing at the busiest checkout ever, my four year old Daughter asked (very loudly) "Mummy do you

remember the first time we went shoplifting together?" And then "Wasn't it fun sitting in the room waiting for the Policeman?" I have no idea where on earth she got this from! It certainly had never happened! I couldn't face anyone, just paid and got out as quickly as possible!
Angela, UK

My Son who was five years old, was in our local shop the other day (we live in a tiny village so everyone knows everyone) and there were five or six other people in the queue with me. My Son then (as loud as ever) asked "Mum can I have some handcuffs?"
"No", I said "We have got enough toys at home."
He just carried on and said "Please Mum they are only plastic."
"No" I said "They are rubbish and they break after one play, put them back." To my shock and horror he then said "Well yours and Daddy's handcuffs don't break and you use them all the time." The looks I got off the people in the shop! One Lady said "You shouldn't let the kids see that." Another one laughed, saying "Never mind love, at least you are having fun." I was mortified! I wouldn't mind but my Son was talking about my Husband's handcuffs from the prison service and they have only ever been out of his bag once to show the kids - I was so embarrassed!
Alison, UK

My Son who was four was sitting next to an elderly Lady on a bus one day, while I was standing with the buggy which my two year old was in. Suddenly My Son shouted "Mummy, this lady has made a noise and really really

really bad smell!" The shade of red I went was not far from a strawberry! The rest of the passengers on the bus were trying to stifle their laughs and the poor old lady was mortified. I didn't know what to do with myself or the children, so I got off at the next stop, not caring that I would have a half hour walk home!
Nina, UK

I took my five year old Cousin shopping once and there was a transsexual Man in front of us in the queue. My Daughter asked very loudly "Why is that Man dressed as a lady?" Not happy with me not answering within two seconds (as I was in complete shock), she directly asked him "Excuse me why are you dressed like a lady?" I could have died with embarrassment. I didn't take her out on my own for a while after that!
Helen, UK

I've got four kids of my own so have endless stories of embarrassing times, but one that stays in my memory is our Daughter coming into the living room when my In Laws were visiting 'smoking' one of my tampons!
Julia, UK

My four year old Son was with me in the queue at the supermarket one day. He saw an elderly Man in the next queue and said (very loudly) "Look at that Man Mum, he's very old isn't he?" Pointing at the poor Man who was hunched over and had a stick. I was already quite embarrassed and answered "Yes Son" When my Son

Laugh Out Loud! Kids

made it worse by asking "He'll be dead soon won't he?" I just wanted the floor to swallow me up!
Vicky, UK

The other day we passed a rather large Lady at the swimming pool and my Son pointed at her and asked "Is that Lady wearing Auntie's body? (My Aunty is a very large lady too!). Luckily the Lady did not seem to mind as she had no idea who my Aunty was!
Janine, UK

We had gone shopping with my Mother In Law once and my Daughter needed the toilet. My Mother In Law took her and whilst they were in the toilets (which were rather full) my Daughter said "Nanny I'm scared" to which she replied "Why?" So my Daughter then pointed at an old slightly hunched over Lady before saying "That Witch is smiling at me." When I heard the tale later I was so glad I wasn't there!
Natalie, UK

When my Daughter was around two, we were in a public toilet somewhere, when the person in the next cubicle let out a loud fart noise. My Daughter instantly asked in the loudest of voices "Has that Lady had done a squishy poo (diarrhea) or a normal poo?" I had never pulled my pants up as fast before and left as quickly as possible so that the poor Lady wouldn't have to see us! How embarrassing!
Alisha, UK

I used to look after my Nephews a lot and had to take the youngest (who was four at the time) shopping with me one day. He was sat in the trolley when a young girl wearing low cut hipsters bent over in front of him to reach something on the bottom shelf and her thong was showing. At the top of his voice my Nephew shouted "That lady flashed her butt at me and she's got holes in her knickers!" I'm not sure who was more embarrassed her or me!
Megan, UK

I was sitting on a bus with my Son one day and he farted very loudly. He immediately looked at me and shouted "Pardon you Mummy!" Obviously I couldn't deny as it would have looked like I was trying to blame him! Ha ha! Thanks darling!
June, UK

I was waiting at the bus stop with my Son and a very small Lady walked past. My Son asked very loudly "Mummy isn't that Lady too little to be out on her own?" I just said "No" as I was not prepared for all the questions which would follow me explaining what 'dwarfism' was. I just hope she didn't hear him!
Maria, UK

I was in Tesco with my seven year old when she tugged my arm and said "Mum, I feel a little uncomfortable here." Thinking she meant uncomfortable as in her shoes hurt or something. I asked her why and she replied (loudly) "That man standing behind us looks really like

that murder man off the news, do you think it's him?" I was mortified and couldn't look round. I had a wee chuckle about it later but I've decided that I need to monitor more closely what she watches on the news!
Kelly, UK

A few years ago I took my Niece who was about three years old at the time to McDonalds as a treat. When carrying the tray to the table we passed this fairly large Lady and my Niece stopped next to her and said very loud and clear "You wouldn't be so fat if you didn't eat all those chips!" I would have just gone out if we hadn't just got our food, so instead, I chose a table as far away from the Lady as possible, I was horrified!"
Katy, UK

The toilets at the supermarket are not very private. My Son was about four when I took him once and he shouted loudly "Mummy are you doing a poo? It stinks!" Thanks dear!
Josie, UK

My Son was two recently and his favourite question is "But why Mummy?" The other day we were in Tesco waiting to pay and he looked up at me and smiled. I asked him "Are you ok?" He replied (loudly) "Yeah Mummy, I done a big big fart. I feel better now!" I could've died! The Guy behind us didn't know where to look!
Mia, UK

We were on a flight home from holiday with our Daughter who was about three at the time. We'd just landed and everyone was stood in the aisles ready to get off the plane, when my Daughter was very sick all over a Lady who was stood up in the aisle! I was mortified! I was rushing to get some wipes for this poor Lady when my Daughter then proceeds to point to the lady's leg and say "Look Mummy, my tea!" (She'd had pasta on the plane for tea which was now all over this Lady's leg!) I didn't know whether to laugh or cry!
Gem, UK

I was starting to run low on some personal things so my Daughter (who had just turned three at the time) and I jumped in the car and went to the local shop. While we were there we picked up everything I needed and some other things. We were standing in the checkout line with this very friendly older Lady who asked my Daughter if she had got anything fun while shopping today. My Daughter said "I just got a new baby." The Lady said "Well that's nice!" My Daughter then said "Mommy got some konex cause her baginia is bleeding." I was so embarrassed I could have ran and never looked back! The Lady just laughed it off and said "Aren't children funny?" Needless to say I now lock the bathroom door!
Jamie, USA

My three year old Son became fixated by his willy and would play with it wherever we went. I tried to explain to him that it wasn't nice to keep touching his willy when he was in public and he seemed to understand. A few days

later we were in a busy supermarket when I noticed my flies were down. As I tried to discreetly sort it out, my Son announced at the top of his voice "Mummy, stop playing with your willy!"
Anya, UK

My Son and I were at the grocery store one day where a Man walked by who obviously had not washed or wore any deodorant that day. I tried to ignore it, hoping my Son wouldn't notice but he did and pointed at the Man, yelling "Mom he stinks and needs a bath!" The store of course was crowded and I turned bright red, grabbed him and started walking away as quickly as I could!
Rita, USA

My Husband and I had just had a satellite dish fitted and were looking through all of our new channels. My Husband thought our little boy (six years old) was in his room and out of earshot when he asked me if we could get the Playboy channel. My Son *was* in earshot however and asked "Mommy what's Playboy?" I couldn't think what to tell him so I said "scary movies." He seemed to accept it and didn't ask any more questions so I left it at that. Later on we watched a movie (a scary one, having completely forgotten what I had said earlier).
The next day we went to my Mom's house and in front of the whole family my Son blurted out "Grandma! Grandma! We were all watching Playboy last night!" My Husband and I were mortified, having to explain that we were not watching Playboy! Next time I'll tell my Son the truth!
Hayley, USA

My Daughter used to think that when grownups kissed they were 'sucking' each other's lips. One day we were in the supermarket and my Daughter was sat in the trolley being pushed by her Dad. I was at the other end of the aisle, all was quiet and I heard her shout "Suck Daddy Mum, suck Daddy!" You can imagine the embarrassment!
Michelle, UK

Once I was at the grocery store, bagging up my groceries with my four kids. My younger Son had just been potty trained, and after a long day shopping with the kids I was going crazy. Just then my Son said "Mommy I have to go potty". I told my older Son to take him to the bathroom, but of course, he just ignored me so I was hurrying trying to bag up all of the food, and I turned around and saw my younger Son walking through the store with his pants and underwear down around his ankles, proclaiming "I went to the bathroom all by myself." I think I about died!
Sasha, USA

I was a Mom of three, my oldest Daughter was three and my twin Daughters were one and a half. We decided as a Family to go grocery shopping because that way if one of the twins went in the opposite direction my Husband could go grab her. As we are making our way through the store the Snack aisle was next. We started at one end, I was looking at the pretzels and my twin Daughters were looking at popcorn and peanuts. Our three year old was standing next to another grocery shopper who also seemed to wants some nuts. So my precious Daughter

Laugh Out Loud! Kids

looked up at her and said "I put my dad's peanus (peanuts) in my mouf (mouth)." Oh Man! My Husband grabbed her little hand and said "Yes honey, you do put Daddy's *peanuts* in your mouth. Your favorites are honey roasted, right?" We left the store quickly and I went back a couple of hours later by myself and started all over!
Martine, USA

My three year old Daughter was drawing a picture in the Doctor's waiting room. She said "Look Mom! A penguin!" I said "Yeah, that's pretty."
She replied "Yeah Mommy, it's a big fat penguin like that girl!" Pointing over to this overweight Woman. I was so embarrassed I couldn't look at anyone in the waiting room, and it was a small waiting room!
Charly, USA

I took my three year old into the dressing room with me while I trying on clothes one day. When I dropped my pants, my underwear went down a little too. My daughter yelled at the top of her lungs "I see your crack, Jack!" I never wanted to leave the dressing room so quickly!
Heather, USA

My Daughter was six when she came to the pet store with me one day. At the checkout in front of us was an elderly Lady. My Daughter, in a pretty loud voice, said to me "Mommy that lady is really crinkly!" (meaning wrinkly). Quietly I tried to tell her it wasn't very nice to talk about people like that, to which she replied "It's ok Mommy,

48

she's old and can't hear me anyways!"
June, USA

Okay, this one is my fault, but it is still funny. I have always tried to teach my Children to eat right, but after my then three year old offered my Aunt (who is diabetic), a piece of candy, she wanted to know why Auntie couldn't eat sweets. I explained to her, (trying to keep it as simple as possible) that if Auntie ate too many sweets, her legs will fall off.
Well, not a week later, we were at the grocery store and the Man in front of us, (who was on crutches and had only one leg) was buying a chocolate bar. My Daughter, without hesitation, went up to him and said "Excuse me mister, but you better not eat that candy unless you want your other leg to fall off too!" I was so embarrassed, I wanted the floor to open up and swallow me!
Joy, USA

While checking out at a store one day, my Son told the cashier "You have such pretty yellow teeth." I was so relieved that the lady appeared not speak English well enough to have caught what he said!
Brianne, USA

I remember telling my camp counsellor once when I was little that her skin was so pretty because it was shiny. I always wondered (until I got older) why she never said thank you!
Laura, USA

My four year old was at story time at the public library and the topic was 'manners'. The Librarian asked the children to call out some examples of good manners. Most of the other kids said, "Say thank you," or "Say please". My son came out with "After you've been digging in your butt you need to wash your hands." I was mortified!
Nariah, USA

My Mom worked at the Pre-school I went to and there was a Lady who was pretty overweight who worked there too. She was talking to my Mom and mentioned that she had to go to the bathroom. I asked "But how do you fit in the bathroom?" with a really concerned look on my face and I was also making wide movements with my hands. There were bathroom stalls at my Pre-school, but they seemed so small and so I couldn't understand how she could get in one. The Lady replied "Just like everybody else." My Mom was extremely embarrassed, but the Lady seemed like she had been asked this question before!
Amanda, USA

My three year old had a UTI and she kept telling me her butt hurt so we went to the Doctor's office. I was pregnant and was suffering with sciatica and had complained a few times to my hubby that my butt hurt. So we were sitting in the waiting room and my Daughter asked loudly (the waiting room was full of people) "Is the Doctor gonna check our butts?" I said "No, honey, he's going to check *your* butt." My Daughter then

asked "Why isn't he going to check *your* butt?" So I replied "Well, my butt doesn't hurt." My Daughter said "Yes it does. You keep telling Daddy it hurts." I was mortified, all the other patients were staring at me, waiting to see what I said next – I kept quiet!
Rhona, USA

When I had my youngest child, my two other children (then aged two and five) went out of the room while the Health Visitor was checking me and the baby over. They reappeared a couple of minutes later with the entire packet of maternity pads stuck to them announcing "We're spacemen!" I couldn't say anything for a while, I was horrified!
Sam, UK

On a busy Saturday afternoon in the supermarket, I had a trolley full of food, a bored four year old, the tills were all open and there were queues snaking everywhere. My four year old picked this moment to point at a nearby lady and ask, extremely loudly "Mummy, why has that lady got a beard?"
I swear the whole supermarket went quiet, you could have heard a pin drop as his chubby little arm proudly pointed to the object of his attentions and I promptly became the object of everyone else's.
With as straight a face as I could muster I answered "Because she wants one."
Shirley, UK

Laugh Out Loud! Kids

My Daughter embarrassed me so much when she was younger but the worst example must have been when she stood up on her chair at my Brother-in-law's big birthday family dinner and shouted "My Mummy has hair on her minky."

I just said "Thank you" and hid my face until someone hastily focused her attention on something else!

Maria, UK

I was out shopping with my little girl and my friend one day and we were in a shoe shop. My friend stayed with my little girl while I had a look around and while I was gone she took off her shoes and put a pair of brand new ones on (which were the exact same shoes) and we left the shop. She was complaining that she couldn't walk properly but being in a rush to get home I just put her in the car and we went.

I didn't realise until we got home that she couldn't walk because the shoes were strapped together with elastic! I told her what she had done was wrong and Mummy could get in trouble. I asked her why she had done it and her reply was "They were cleaner."

Obviously I took the 'new' shoes back to the shop and apologised!

Allie, UK

Kids Know Best:-

Although we are the adults, our children sometimes (or most of the time) think they know better than we do, how to do things, what to say etc. and they will happily tell us so!

When my little girl was five we were trying to get her to stop using a dummy when she went to bed. The first dummy free night we left a little gift and a handwritten note from the 'fairies' in her bedroom. In the morning she came running through, waving the note at me. I said to her "Wow! What does it say?" She said "I don't know, I can't read it, the writing's too curly" then shook her head, frowned and said "The fairies really should buy a computer Mummy." Ha Ha!
Jessica, UK

I was trying to get my Son to say "I love Mammy" so I was saying to him "Mammy loves you" and then saying "You love ...." and pausing for him to fill in the gap. Well the answers I got were "Teddy", "Mickey Mouse" and "Giraffe." That'll teach me to fish for compliments!
Natalie, UK

My Daughter was pulling a pile of books in their case around by the string. I thought she was playing a game and asked "Is that your doggy you're taking for a walk?" she replied very matter of fact "No, it's a pile of books mummy." I couldn't help laughing at the look she gave me!
Hayley, UK

I said to my six year old Niece one day that she had a really pretty dress on and then I asked her where she got it from. She looked at me, frowned and replied "My wardrobe."
Silly me, where else would you get a dress from?
Tania, UK

This happened to my sister in law. She was shopping in a local clothes shop where the assistants (all sisters) happen to be larger ladies, and my Nephew, then about four, asked loudly, "Mummy, do you have to be fat to work here?" How embarrassing! My sister in law couldn't get out the door quick enough!
Natalie, UK

My Son and I were on a bus, sitting opposite a lady who had a large mole on her face. He just stared at it, I did everything to try to distract him and was relieved when we got to our stop with no comment, or so I thought! As we walked to get off he gently put his hand on the ladies knee and asked with great concern, "You won't pick that

spot now will you?" I was so glad we were getting off!
Nina, UK

My Daughter threw her teddy on the floor in her bedroom so I tried to show her that it wasn't nice. I said "Poor teddy, he wants a cuddle, don't throw him on the floor." to which my Daughter replied "Mum, it's a stuffed toy." That's me told then!
Sonia, UK

My Husband's car went to the garage for a service the other day and my Daughter asked where it was, so I said "It has gone to a special car hospital." My son then corrected me by saying "No Mum, it's called a garage!" He looked at me as if I had lost my mind!
Brenda, UK

We were watching a children's programme this morning on TV and I was trying to see how much my Son was listening to it and learning from it so I was asking "What colour is the frog?" And "Is that a big frog, or a little frog?" etc so when it came to "What kind of frog is that?" He looked at me like I was really stupid and said "A Bullfrog Mummy, the TV lady just told you that" whilst rolling his eyes at me! I was in bits and he just kept saying "It's not funny Mummy - you need to listen." This obviously just set me off laughing even more!
Jane, UK

Laugh Out Loud! Kids

My little girl is three, and in a bid to keep her awake the other day on the way home from Nursery we were discussing what everyone had in their packed lunch. When I asked what she had had, she replied "Don't be silly Mummy, you made it so you know what was in there." I couldn't stop laughing, cheeky madam!
Rachel, UK

We were at the Doctors once and my Daughter stayed in the waiting room with her Daddy when it was my turn to go in. As I stood up and opened the door, she shouted "She's *my* Mummy, you can borrow her, but just for a minute." The rest of the waiting room thought it was hilarious!
Em, UK

My Daughter once ran up to the Nurse after I had just had some blood taken and asked "Can you not put that plaster on my Mummy's arm again, it hurts." She then went on to say to the nurse "At home we have Mr Men and Princess ones, you should get some, *they* don't hurt." The Nurse of course agreed to take her advice!
Val, UK

I was sat on my front porch one day and I saw a stray dog run past me. I was worried it might get hit by a car and so I was calling it, trying to get it to come over. My two year old Daughter was inside so I couldn't leave the porch and go after it. Just then my Daughter came to the door and asked "Mommy? You out-yide by yousef?" I said "Yeah I'm outside by myself." She then asked me "Well den oo you takin to, silly?" I felt so stupid for walking into that one!

Later that day she started playing with my purse and she knows she's not supposed to. I asked "Hey what are you doing? I can see you!" Her response was "If you can see me why do you have to ask?"

Terry, USA

One day I was apparently 'nagging' a bit too much. While I was talking to my Husband, my four year old piped up and said "Daddy, don't listen to her, she's crazy!" Thanks Son!

Julie, UK

"It was Christmas morning and my Daughter thought I hadn't got any presents. She said "You must not have been a good girl if Santa didn't bring you anything." I said "I must not have been." She asked me "Are you going to try harder for next year?" I told her I was and she replied with "You probably shouldn't yell at me anymore Mom. That would be a good start." I almost peed my pants laughing!

Brianne, USA

I was pregnant with my third child and my two year old Son kept standing up in his chair at the kitchen table while eating his breakfast. I repeatedly told him to sit down so he wouldn't fall and get hurt. Of course he would sit and get right back up and I was on my last nerve being pregnant and sick and I looked at him and asked, "Why can't you just listen to Mommy, please?" He looked at me

said "Cuz I'm poopin!" I couldn't help but laugh. That was the reason he wouldn't sit down!
Lorna, USA

I was getting my two year old Son out of his wet clothes after playing in the snow when I said "Hey, your bum is cold" He replied "I know, I had it outside wis me!" So Cute!
Trish, UK

When my Nephew was about 4 he was told to go to bed by his visiting Grandfather. His reply was "That's OK Grandpa, I slept yesterday."
Olivia, USA

My two year old Son woke up one morning, came into the living room and asked for something to eat. I asked him, "What would you like for breakfast?" to which he replied (very seriously), "Food." Well I never!
Ruby, UK

My Son has recently taken to patting my belly and saying, "More babies, please!" When I finally asked him *why* he wants more babies he said, "Sister's getting bigger now." Our Daughter will be one soon, and we had been talking about how it won't be long until she's not a baby anymore, so my Son figures it's time to have another!
Sophie, UK

I had a huge project due and unfortunately for a week I spent more time at the kitchen table doing this than playing with my two year old Daughter. About a week later, my Husband and I were trying to make up for 'lost' time with her and had found that there was a grand opening of a new kid gym in town. We presented the idea to our Daughter by asking "Would you like to go to a jungle place to jump around and meet some new kids?" Without even looking up (she was playing with playdough) she said with such an honest tone "Could you be patient, please? I'm kinda busy right now." My Husband had to go out of the room, he was laughing so much.
Grace, USA

My Grandpa was teasing my Daughter, trying to get her to say that Nana was bad. So he said to her "Go tell Nana she's bad." Without skipping a beat she pipes up with "No Poppa, you're bad. You want a time out?" We all almost peed our pants laughing. Nana still uses it against him!
Ava, USA

My Son very rarely eats meat, and one day after lunch I was cleaning him up and was asking him why he wouldn't just eat his chicken and why he never eats meat. "Try anything." I said "A hot dog, a cheeseburger, just something other than strawberries and bananas." He looked at me with the most serious face and said "I'm a fruit kinda guy, okay?"
Katie, USA

Laugh Out Loud! Kids

My Daughter (then four years old) was learning about how plants grew in Pre-school. We were driving down the road one day, and she asked "Mommy, do you know why that tree isn't growing?" I asked her why and she said, "Cause it has no water." I then asked her, "Do you know what makes us grow?" She replied, "Birthdays, duh!"
Summer, USA

My eight year old twin girls were playing together at the kitchen table one day. I overheard their conversation from the other room:
Twin 1: "Ew! Get your finger out of your nose!"
Twin 2: "But there's something in there!"
Twin 1: "Duh! Its' your finger!"
This made me giggle, although I didn't let on I could hear them.
Freya, USA

My Niece came home from School one day with an art project. It was a brown glob with specs of other colors in it, made out of clay. When my Sister asked what it was she said "Duh Mumma! It's a dog poop!" We both had no answer for that one!
Hannah, USA

I had just put my Son to bed and said "Goodnight sweetie pie." His reply to me was "I'm not a pie." I tried to explain that he was my cute little sweetie pie but he was having none of it, insisting he was not a pie!
Isla, USA

The other day, my Daughter told me that there was probably no such thing as the 'Tooth Fairy' since grownups could sneak into their room, take and hide the tooth, then print a letter off the computer (busted!) She was also the one who informed me that of course you can't catch a bus because you would need a gigantic net!
Helen, UK

My four year old wanted a dress she saw on a cartoon character. I told her that dress wasn't real because it was a cartoon. Her response was "Santa has everything. He can bring it to me."
Shanna, UK

A few of my Family and I were watching 'Finding Nemo'. My Daughter kept asking questions and my Husband asked "Why do you ask so many questions?" She replied "Because that's what little girls do Daddy!" Ha Ha!
Melanie, UK

At my baby shower recently my friend asked my Son "How old are you now?"
He replied "six, I'm practically a teenager." Everyone laughed!
Sheena, UK

My little girl fell down and skinned her knee on the sidewalk in front of our house. I took her inside to clean

up her knee and I said, "Poor baby. Do you want Mommy to kiss your knee and make it better?"
She said, "Mommy, my knee will feel better if you kiss it, but I'm not a baby, I'm a Woman!" She's four!
Miley, USA

Telling Tales and Getting Parents In Trouble:-

We tell our kids off if they do something they shouldn't, so why wouldn't they do the same if they see *us* doing something *they* think we shouldn't be doing? They are always listening (especially when we think they aren't) and they like to choose just the right time to repeat what they have heard!

My Son only really says one word or phrase at a time but its the context in which he says them that cracks me up, for example my Mother In Law came round the other day (she comes round most nights although I would rather she didn't!) As soon as my Son saw her he said "Oh God" and face palmed! Ha Ha!
Emmy, USA

We live in a small village where everyone knows everyone else's business. I was in the local shop and the Shopkeeper asked my Daughter "Are you a big girl?"
She said "Yes, I don't cry, I'm a big girl, but Mummy cries in the cupboard." I do not! I have no idea where she got this from but now everyone looks at me as if I'm strange!
Amanda, UK

My Daughter has started telling on people. Yesterday when I picked her up from Nursery she said "Mummy, me had bit Daddy's pizza for breakfast!" followed by a shocked face! He had obviously told her not to tell!
Sharon, UK

My Husband had been trying to use the 'time out' technique with our eldest one day while I was out. When I came home and asked what they had got up to, my eldest piped up as happy as could be with "I've been playing 'naughty corners' with Dad but he wasn't very good as he kept losing" Oh dear, poor Dad!
Molly, UK

Apparently when I was about three or four I was at my Grandparents house and dropped my ice cream, and exclaimed "Oh f***!" Then I stopped, and said "Whoops, only Daddies can say that!" Both my Grandparents were very proper but cracked up at this one!
Charlene, UK

One day, we were at the lake. My Daughter (who was four at the time) really had to go to the bathroom so I said "Just go in the lake, its fine, but go in a little deeper." She went in the lake, turned to me and screamed "Mom, is it deep enough for me to pee yet?" All eyes were on me, I didn't know where to look!
Tammy, USA

I was driving down the street, hurrying because my Son was late for soccer. I was pulled over for speeding. The officer asked me if I had been drinking, and of course I answered "no." To that, my 5 year old who was sitting in the back screamed "Yes, she was! I saw her drink!" I was drinking a can of soda earlier!
Esther, USA

I teach a class of seven year old children and I asked what they thought of beer. Here are their responses (names removed):-

1. "I think beer must be good. My Dad says the more beer he drinks the prettier my Mom gets."

2. "Beer makes my Dad sleepy and we get to watch what we want on television when he is asleep, so beer is nice."

3. "My Mom and Dad both like beer. My Mom gets funny when she drinks it and takes her top off at parties, but Dad doesn't think this is very funny."

4. "My Mom and Dad talk funny when they drink beer and the more they drink the more they give kisses to each other, which is a good thing."

5. "My Dad gets funny on beer. He is funny. He also wets his pants sometimes, so he shouldn't have too much."

6. "My Dad loves beer. The more he drinks, the better he dances. One time he danced right into the pool."

7. "I don't like beer very much. Every time Dad drinks it, he burns the sausages on the barbecue and they taste disgusting."

Anonymous, USA

Cheeky But Funny Comments and Attitude:-

We've all been there, your child says something really cheeky but instead of telling them off you end up going into another room so they can't see you laughing!

My Daughter comes out with some crackers, some are not exactly funny though. The other morning she said "Mummy put your make up on, make it all better!" Cheeky little monkey!
Beverley, UK

Last week my washing machine was broken so I took my washing to give to my Mum and my Daughter said to me "Mummy, why are you treating your Mum like a servant?" She also tells me "Shh, I'm concentrating" all the time Ha Ha!
Hayley, UK

My Son's favourite thing at the moment is to fart then say

Laugh Out Loud! Kids

"Oh pooh, Mummy." I don't think so! Little tinker!
Deb, UK

My Daughter keeps saying 'Hello, I'm the Queen, bow when you speak to me!"
Mary, UK

This morning's conversation with my Daughter:
Her: "Mummy shower!"
Me: "Why, what's wrong, does mummy smell?"
Her: "Mummy smells, bad!"
Donna, UK

My nine year old was playing outside with her baby doll. She had to run into the house and get something so she handed me the doll and said "Here Mommy, you need practice taking care of a baby." I started cracking up as I told her "I took care of you and you're fine!"
Bree, USA

When I had my 4D scan the other day I was laying there happily watching my boy and my Daughter turned to me and said, "look Mummy, he's going to be fat like you!" Charming!
Leah, UK

The other day I was out driving with my Mum and Daughter. My Daughter wanted to look at herself in the mirror, but my Mum was in her way so she said "I want to

look in the mirror Granny, move, move your fat head!" I explained that we do not speak to Granny like that, but I had to stop myself laughing first!
Mia, UK

I was putting my Son into his car seat and he pointed to my chest and said out of the blue "They your boobs!"
I said: "Yes, they're my boobs"
He said: "I poke them?"
I said: "Um, no, poke your own boobs."
He said: "No, silly Mummy!"
Charlotte, UK

When my Daughter was three, one day she played me up in a shop because I wouldn't buy her a toy she wanted. That night I tucked her into bed as usual and said "I was very sad with you for running away in the shop today, that was naughty. What do you think you should say?" She replied "I'm sorry Mummy, now what do *you* say for not buying that toy?"
Heather, UK

We went to the drive through before going to the playground yesterday. The people in front of us didn't order anything, they were just at the window chatting, it was odd. Then when we finally did get to the window, the girl took our payment and stood there and talked to the other girl about what we ordered, etc. They were obviously on a shift change, but were taking forever.
The girl opened the window with my Son's milk, and we're regulars there, so she decided to greet my son, as usual.

She asked "Is this for you, sweetie?" So he responded, in his robot voice, "Me a robot." She said "You're a robot today." He replied, still in his robot voice, "Robot wants you to hurry up."
I could've died. It was so rude, but I wanted to laugh (plus I agreed with him). So I turned around and told him "That wasn't nice, she is trying her best." When she came back to the window, he told her "I'm sorry my robot said that. He's really really rude" in his normal voice!
Samantha, USA

I was looking after my friends two year old a few months back and it was lunch time. I always make sure she uses her manners so when she demanded "Give me my juice" I promptly replied "Say that again, properly please." I expected her response to be "Give me my juice please" but instead I got "Give me my juice, Aunty."
It melted my heart hearing her call me that and I was pretty much wrapped round her finger for the rest of the afternoon!
Katy, UK

While shopping in a supermarket the other day, we had tried some samples of strawberries and cream. My youngest obviously liked his and said to the Lady giving out the samples (with his hand outstretched) "More now please Lady." I told him he was only supposed to have one, but the Lady was so amused she gave him some more!
Anna, UK

My two year old decided she didn't want peas the other day, but I put them on her plate anyway. When I put the plate in front of her she shouted "Mummy, peas off!" I laughed so much I cried!
Jodie, UK

We took our kids to a drive through restaurant for a treat just last week and we had got our drinks and were waiting for the food when our nearly four year old shouted at the serving girl "Oi love, where's my burger?" I was howling, it was very cheeky of her but I couldn't help but laugh at the time!
Carla, UK

My Niece had been toilet trained and it soon came to the time her Mum thought she should be able to wipe herself. My Niece looked concerned but her mum showed her the best way to be thorough, and all seemed well, until the following day when once again my Niece reverted to the "I'm finished" call to her Mum.
"But you can do it all by yourself now" points out Mum.
"Eeeww yes, but I don't want to do this smelly job for the rest of my life!" Was the reply!
Keira, UK

At the weekend, my 4 year old said to my really fit and active 74 year old Dad, "Papa, you're really old, but you're still alive." Should he take this as a compliment? I'm not sure!
Lisa, UK

Laugh Out Loud! Kids

I am always asking my Son what things are, what colour etc. Most of the time he replies "You should know that Mummy, you're a grown up" and walks off!
Kelly, UK

My three year old had me in stitches yesterday, he trumped then the little monkey said "Eww that stinks Mummy, that must be you!" I think he's turning into a proper little man already!
Angela, UK

I had just been in the bath and my Daughter, four years old, saw me getting dressed and said "Oooh gross! Why is your butt naked?"
I replied "Hey! I don't say 'ooh gross' when I see your naked hiney" and she quickly replied "Yeah but *my* hiney's cute!"
Stacey, USA

I'm not sure where this has come from but whenever I do something my Son is not impressed by he says "You're fired!" Whenever he says it everyone else bursts out laughing.
Debbie, USA

My Daughter was 5 and very upset with me because she didn't want to leave her Auntie's house. My Brother In Law was just coming in the door from work. He growled at my Daughter (like a monster noise). She put her hands

on her hips and told him very sternly, "I am not in any kind of mood to be growled at. Please do not do that anymore." We all just about died laughing!
Tammy, USA

My charming three year old Daughter told her Father last week after he took her to the dentist "Daddy, I am really tired of you right now, can you take me to Mommy?" When we ask her to do something we get "Sorry, I can't. I am kinda busy at the moment" then we insist she does as she has been asked we get "Fine, Have it your way. This is so not fair" When did my three year old become a teenager?
Gemma, USA

My friend was saying to her five year old that Mummy was a bit tired as she had been up with her baby Sister in the night a few times. The five year old said "Well you shouldn't have had another baby then!" Kids are so astute!
Sarah, UK

My Daughter has just turned five. She was in a really bad mood the other day, and I asked her why. She said "It's not fair, whenever I ask you or Daddy to take me somewhere, you always say no!" I couldn't understand what she meant.
"Like where? "I asked.
She shocked me when she said "Like America!"
How badly we treat her!
Ruby, UK

A few months ago I burned a baked potato in the microwave (this involved a small fire which I extinguished). My Daughter then said "I think you need to work on being a better Mother!"
Kate, UK

Just the other day my three year old didn't want to go to Day care and we told her she couldn't stay home alone. She informed us "I won't be alone, 'Dora' will watch me!"
Ella, USA

I was getting our Son some yoghurt last night and apparently I was taking too long because he looked at me and said "This is ridiculous!" I could not help but laugh!
Caroline, USA

My Partner was scolding our three year old Daughter the other day and she put her hand up and said, "Dude, calm down." We had to go in the other room so she couldn't see us laughing!
Felicity, USA

My Son, almost four was playing with his Aunty and got a bit excited and ran and jumped on her a bit too hard so I asked him to say sorry. He kissed her stomach and went to walk off so I asked him again to say sorry (he has a habit of not actually saying the word). Once again he kissed her on the belly and went to walk off. Again I

asked for him to say sorry, this time he gave her a cuddle, so I said "Thank you for giving Auntie a cuddle but can you please say sorry?" He just looked at me blankly so I took my Sister's hand and showed him how to do it. He said "Sorry Aunty."
"Thank you" she replied. He turned around and started walking off and muttered "I'm not sorry." Little monkey!
Alison, UK

My Daughter is almost three and likes to broadcast to the world whilst sitting in the shopping trolley. This week it was "Attention Ladies and Gentleman! I have a scratch on my bottom" in her loudest voice. Also this week she has cracked her first joke "What noise does a dog make? 'Woof', what noise does a cat make? 'Meow', what noise does a duck make? Quack, what noise does a bum make? Trump!" She thinks this is hilarious although most of the time it's just embarrassing!
Pauline, UK

Before my three year old was potty trained, we would always tell him he owed us a kiss every time we changed a stinky nappy. My Husband had just finished cleaning him up after one such nappy and my Son was just about to turn and run when my Husband asked "Hey, how 'bout a kiss?"
My son replied "How 'bout a cookie?"
Sammy, UK

My Son is always making me laugh with his cheeky humour, here are a couple of examples:-

Me: "Can you go to bed now? It's bed time."
My Son: "No!"
Me: "I am the Mummy, I make the rules."
My Son: "No Mummy, I make the rules - you make the dinner!"

Another time he was running through the hall with a cheeky grin and said "Mum, you will have to buy some more of your chocolates at the shop."
"Why?" I said "I've only had about four."
He said "Yeah, but I've had lots."
Jenna, UK

My Daughter has just learned to burp on command (not taught by me!) The other day I said "We need to go and get some gas."
She said "Here's your gas" and did a whopping great burp in my face! It's hard to tell her off when you're in fits of giggles!
Lindsey, USA

Observations and Understanding of a Child:-

We try to teach our children what things are, how they work etc. but sometimes they get a little confused along the way and create their own ideas. They are always watching and aren't afraid to tell us their latest observation, proudly explaining what they've seen (preferably with an audience)!

My Daughter had been in the bathroom with her Dad while I was cooking dinner. She came running up to me shortly afterwards shouting "Mummy! Daddy has a carrot growing out of his front bum!" Daddy went bright red as he tried to explain it wasn't a carrot! Ha Ha!
Julie, UK

My Son has taken to pointing at my lady area when I get out of the shower lately and proudly declaring "brush!" Thanks Son.
I know it's untidy, I'm pregnant though so back off! Ha Ha!
Samia, UK

My three year old Daughter asked me "Why does Daddy have an elephant trunk?"
I said "It's not a trunk!" Then had to try to explain the whole boy/girl thing!
Claire, UK

I was trying to get my Daughter to understand the difference between a girl and a boy so I said something like "You are a big girl, Daddy is a big boy" and so on. She seemed to be getting the hang of it then we got to Granny I said "Granny is a big?"
She said "Elephant!" I was laughing so hard you wouldn't believe!
Tina, UK

My Son likes to follow everyone to the toilet at the moment. The other morning he followed me into the bathroom and while I was sat on the loo he noticed I was wearing a pad in my knickers. After looking at it for a while, he looked up at me with a strange expression and said "Mammy wearing a nappy? Babies wear nappies, not Mammies." I just agreed with him, I was not having a conversation about why I was wearing it that day!
Heather, UK

I had my Daughter drop a few food pellets in the bowl for her fish. They fell to bottom and she said, after watching them not eating for a few minutes "Dumb fish, you gotta eat so you don't die!" I was laughing so much!
Hayley, USA

This was a conversation with my six year old the other day:-

Him: "I'm the cutest, then you, Mom, then Daddy."
Me: "Really? Well, I think Lucy is the cutest."
Him: "But Lucy is just a kitty!"
Me: "You're just a little boy."
Him: "You're just an old Woman!"

I was twenty six at the time, and apparently old!
Shauna, USA

When I first had my twins, I found it really hard to have any quality one to one time with my eldest Son, who had just turned four. I said to him "Don't forget, we have not one, but two babies to look after now and its hard work and makes Mummy very tired." He promptly replied "Let's just give one away then!"
Thankfully he's grown out of that idea and loves his Brothers to pieces now!
Jennifer, UK

Once My Aunty was telling my Cousin off when he was little and she said "It's about time you learned to pull your socks up." He thought about this for a few seconds and then bent down and pulled his socks up! My Aunty didn't carry on telling him off, she was laughing too much!
Aimee, UK

I was talking to my Son about what his Daddy did as his job. I asked my Son what job he wanted when he was older. After thinking long and hard his reply was "I want to be a Power Ranger." Then he thought for a few more seconds and said "Or Sonic!"
He asked me, rather hurt, why I was laughing at him – he was very serious about his future!
Emma, UK

I am a Teaching Assistant. One of the kids asked me one day "Do you have any kids?"
I said "No, I don't have any kids."
Her reply was "Oh, what about Grandkids then?"
Another one wanted to know how old I was so I said "Really old."
He asked "Are you thirteen then?"
They make me laugh every day!
Jane, UK

When my Son and Daughter were toddlers my Son asked "How does a Doctor know the difference between boys and girls?"
I asked him "What have you got that your Sister hasn't?"
His reply, after a short pause, was "Short hair." I made sure I explained to him the real difference!
Emily, UK

My six year old Nephew was visiting with us last week and we had this conversation:-
Me: "Do you love your Aunty?" (Me)
Nephew: "Not sure, do you like 'Phineas and Ferb'?"

Me: "Yeah."
Nephew: "Do you like 'Ben Ten and The Green Lantern?'"
Me: "Yeah"
Nephew: "Well, I guess I love you then."
He is such a funny little dude!
Teresa, USA

My Niece was with her other Grandma recently and asked "Nana why are you so fat?"
Her Mum was horrified so said "You can't say things like that!"
She replied "Why not? She *is* really fat!"
Gemma, UK

Yesterday we went to the 'Crackerbarrel' for lunch with my folks. As we were pulling up my three year old said to me "Mommy, I like crackers but I don't like barrels" Got to love toddler logic!
Aubrey, USA

I have a friend named Tyrell, My son calls him "The Bell," but reminds me every once in a while that he really isn't a bell, he's a guy!
Fatima, USA

I was getting dressed the other day and my two year old Daughter brought me my bra and shouted "Boobs! Put in bra!" She was very proud that she showed me what to do!
Fiona, UK

I was playing a kids trivia game with my six year old Son yesterday and he asked the question "Who lives at The Vatican?" My Son read the answer and said "Popeye!" Then he told everyone "I'm very clever, just like 'Alan Titchmarsh!'" We later found out he meant 'Albert Einstein.' Those two aren't quite the same!
Mandy, UK

I was at my Sister's house one night when she said to her Son "Ok, bed time now."
To which he replied "I can't go to bed Mum. I'm allergic of the dark."
Lacey, UK

I was washing up once and my Son came in to me and asked "Mum, why do you have to pay for babies?"
I was shocked and replied "What? You don't have to pay for babies."
He said "Yes you do, I know you do, because when a baby comes you say they're seven pound something." I could not stop laughing!
Eve, UK

When my Son was about four, he walked in on my Husband in the shower. He came out looking sheepish and worried and told me it was because "Daddy hasn't got a winky, he's got a thing with fur on it!"
Susan, UK

When my Daughter was five she asked her Granny "How old are you?"
Granny replied "I'm so old I don't remember any more."
My Daughter advised her "If you don't remember, you must look in the back of your panties. Mine say five to six."
Ruby, USA

My Cousin, when she was around four was drinking juice when she got the hiccups. She said to her Mom "Please don't give me this juice again, it makes my teeth cough."
Carol, USA

I am dieting at the moment and have scales in the bathroom. My four year old Son was in there with me the other day and stood on them asking "How much do I cost?" So cute!
Sylvia, UK

My five year old Son was in his bedroom looking worried one day. When I asked what was wrong, he replied, "My bed is too small!" I asked him what he meant and said "You have plenty of room in there."
He said "Yes but what about when I get married? How will my wife fit in it?" I told him he didn't need to worry about that for a while yet! I really don't know where this came from!
Marley, USA

I used to work in a shoe shop so I was used to measuring kid's feet. One little boy who I'm guessing was around four or five, came up to me and asked "Excuse me Lady, can you weigh my feet?"
"Of course I can sweetie." I said, trying my best not to laugh!
Mya, USA

I asked my Daughter what job she wanted to do when she was older and she said "When I grow up I want to be the person who sits behind the wall giving money to people when they put their card in. I will get paid with what's left over." I love that they have their own logic!
Nat, UK

My Son asked me the other day "Mom, when we get older how will we know where to find you?"
I started to explain that he will always know where I will be, etc. when he said "Oh, I know! GPS!"
Denise, USA

I was eating oranges the other day and I was telling my nineteen year old niece how much I loved them and my five year old Son pipes up with tears in his eyes "Does that mean you're gonna leave Daddy?" I couldn't help but laugh and give him a big hug and reassure him that I wasn't leaving his Daddy for an orange!
Hannah, UK

My Niece made me laugh one day. My Brother In Law was eating a bowl of ice cream and my Niece (who was two at the time) said "Eat it before it gets cold."
He said "It's already cold."
She replied "Eat it before it gets hot then!" Love their Logic!
Rhianna, UK

I once got mad at my Mom for putting on a 'Roy Orbison' record and telling
me she loved him. I looked at her all mad and asked "And does Daddy know 'bout this?"
Freya, USA

My son was six when he was carrying his pet turtle around after the bowl had been cleaned and when he put him back inside, he was staring at it for a while and announced "This is a female turtle!"
I asked him "How can you tell?" (I was a little worried he would say something where I would have to explain the birds and the bees to him afterwards).
His reply was "Well Mom, I know it's a female turtle because it just winked at me!"
Amanda, USA

My Son totally embarrassed me the other day with his people watching when we were out shopping. He pointed over at an elderly Lady and asked "Why has that old Lady got wrinkly skin? Has she been in the bath too long?" I did find it funny when we got home and I didn't

have to feel the old Lady's stare!
Marie, UK

My five year old Daughter saw a homeless Man sitting in the subway by where we live, she asked "Why is he there?"
I said "He has no home."
She replied "If *we* have no home, do we have to go sit next to him?"
Anna, USA

I was sat in the Doctor's waiting room with my four year old Niece while her Mum was being seen. My Niece was busy colouring, but then looked up at me and very seriously stated "You have polka dots on your face." The whole room just burst in to laughter. I was wondering if my freckles were getting darker since I've been pregnant or if it was just my imagination, I guess not!
Tanya, UK

One of my Mom's foster kids came up to me with a washcloth the other day and said "Here, a little water should get that off" whilst rubbing at my tattoo! I explained that it didn't come off!
Jade, USA

When my Cousin was younger she asked my Mum "Where's Mummy?"
Mum replied "On the computer." So she went to have a look and then came back in to my Mum, shouting "Nanny,

she is on the chair, not the computer!" We were in stitches for ages!
Rebecca, UK

I'm a Teaching Assistant and one day all the children went to a farm while I stayed behind. When they came back they were telling me how the trip went. One of them said "We saw some cows, they were playing."
I said "Oh right."
Then another child said "They were giving each other a piggy back." I was laughing so much!
Lesley, UK

My three year old is always asking where things come from lately so last week I was asking her "Where do eggs come from?"
She said "Chickens."
I asked "Where does milk come from?"
She said "Cows, goats and Mummies." Ha Ha!
Lorraine, UK

My Daughter is a bit older now and has started to ask about Men's 'bits.' I was in the bath and she was sitting close by, speaking to me. She asked me "Why are Men different from Women down there?" (pointing to her bits).
I asked "How come you want to know?"
She said "Oh I was in the bath one time and Daddy needed a wee wee really bad. He said to me to turn around and don't look so I did, but I had a sneak peek."
I said "Oh, ok."

She said "Yeah, he had a huge nose poking out of a hairy beard down there."
"Oh, did he?" Was all I could manage before I burst out laughing!
Jenna, UK

We were getting a movie rental one day and I had my four year old Niece with me. The cashier scanned my membership card and said "Thank you, Madam, the rental has to be back for Sunday night."
My Niece suddenly said "Her name is not Madam, its Aunty Rachel!"
Rachel, USA

My Cousin was telling me that her Daughter (who is three) asked her Dad if he had boobies and he told her he did but they were different than hers. Then she asked my Cousin if *she* had boobies, and she said "Yes." Then my Daughter said "Whoa Mommy, you got a whole lot of boobies!"
Shianne, USA

When my Niece was about three she was watching a programme about fish. She told her Mum that she didn't like fish, and my Sister said "Yes you do, you eat fish fingers."
She replied "I know but that's proper fish."
My sister asked her "What are the fish on the TV if they aren't proper fish?"
My Niece responded with "They are sea creature fish."
Catherine, UK

A few weeks after my Daughter was born, my Son who was two years old, was in dire need of Mommy time. This was how our conversation went:-
Me: "Are you Mama's baby?"
Son: "Nope."
Me: "Are you Mama's big boy?"
Son: "Hmm....nope!"
Me: "Then what are you honey?"
Son: "I'm me Mommy!"
Carrie, USA

My Son, who is four really makes me laugh with his sayings. His latest one was "Mummy, I don't need my head to think. I can do it with my mouth, and my nose."
Natasha, UK

My Son would not finish his dinner as he said he was "filled up."
I told him "That's fine." He then asked for a yoghurt. I said to him "I thought you were 'filled up' and he replied "But there is still a little room in my toes." Little Monkey!
Lisa, USA

I remember watching the weather forecast and it said there was heavy snow on its way "Oh, it's gonna be heavy snow tomorrow" I said to my Hubby.
My Son replied "Oh no! Does that mean we won't be able to pick it up to make snowmen?"
Joy, USA

My Hubby's friend is nicknamed 'Woody.' My Son asked "What's Woody's second name?"
I said "Wood."
He looked at me and said "Woody Wood, what sort of a name is that?" I rolled about laughing obviously he's called 'Woody' because 'Wood' is his surname, not his first name too!
Lara, UK

I remember once my little Brother was in a shop with my older Brother (there is a large age gap between them). My younger Brother was about three years old and just pulled his trousers and pants down, and my Older Brother was mortified and said "What do you think you're doing?" My Younger Brother said, really loud and stroppy, "I have a wedgie." He's not lived it down to this day!
Gail, USA

My five year old Daughter told me the other day "Mummy, we shouldn't touch bees because they have bottoms that sting, but they are not like our bottoms because they don't have a line." Ha Ha!
Heidi, UK

I was out with my five year old Daughter shopping for a Christening present for a friend's Daughter. We were in a jewelers when my Daughter asked what a Christian was (we are not religious), so I explained. She then turned to me and said "Mummy when I grow up I don't want to be a

Christian, I want to be a Teacher as they get loads of holidays!" I and the Women behind the counter were crying with laughter!
Debbie, UK

I was walking down the street one day with my three year old Daughter. She pointed to some berries on a bush, and I said to her "You can't eat them because they are poisonous." We carried on and saw some orange berries. My Daughter said "They boys nuts Mummy."
I said "Yes darling" with a little chuckle and we carried on when we came to some red berries and she said "They girls nuts Mummy." Oh children are so funny!
Jo, UK

Our Son told us last week that "Granddad is getting old now cos his cheeks are dropping." I'm so glad that Granddad wasn't there when he said it!
Karla, UK

I don't get much privacy in the bathroom from my four year old Daughter whether I'm using the loo or the shower. I was showering a few weeks ago and asked my Daughter what she was doing lying on the floor and she replied, laughing, "Mummy, you have a bottom beard!" Oh, the joy of kids! It did make me laugh though.
Nina, UK

My six year old Son has just told me that I'm trying to turn him into a girl, making him have a bath and clean his

Laugh Out Loud! Kids

teeth! He thinks boys should be allowed to be dirty all the time!
Kealey, UK

My Daughter was ill one day and I had to go to work so I took her to my Mom who spent the day looking after her for me. I was worried about her so after about an hour I phoned my Mom to see if my Daughter was okay. I had a word with my Daughter and she was feeling much better. I was then speaking to my Mom who reassured me by saying "Stop worrying, it will have just been a twenty four hour bug." My Daughter heard this and I heard her in the background screaming "No Nana! I haven't been eating any bugs!" Me and my Mom cracked up and I will be telling that story at her wedding one day!
Sasha, USA

My Son kept saying "I want to play in the jungle." I thought he meant a game he was playing but then he pointed outside to our garden! It was a bit overgrown at the time!
Emma, UK

Last weekend, my Husband, Parents, Daughter and I were passing the high school that my four year old will eventually go to. I pointed it out to her and said "It's near Granny and Papa's house, so you'll be able to run down to their house for lunch." She quickly replied "I'll probably have my own car by then, so I'll drive there." We were all in stitches but hope it's not a sign of the demands she'll

be making in the future!
Steph, UK

I was visiting the Zoo with my Mom and Grandma when I was little. We were walking by the gorillas, and all of a sudden, I put my hands on the glass, and screamed really loudly and excitedly, "Daddy!" Everyone was laughing. I guess I wasn't embarrassed at the time, but they haven't let me live it down! I don't know why I would have said it as my Dad doesn't look like a gorilla!
Evie, USA

My five year old Son was screaming in the back yard one night while he was playing and all of the sudden this voice yells, "Be Quiet!"
My Son ran in, shocked. He looked at me and said, "Mom I think that was God, I better be quiet."
Dee, USA

When my Son was three and we were in a toy shop. He walked past something and it fell over. I said "Hey!"
He looked at me and said "It wasn't my fault! It was unstable!"
I couldn't believe he said that at three years old. I thought it was hilarious!
Marie, UK

At our house, the bathroom may as well not have a door. No matter who is using it or what they are doing, my three year old Son comes in. It was 'that' time of the

month for me and I was using the bathroom. My Son walked in and I asked him if I could have some privacy. He said "Yes Mom" and shut the bathroom door. I said "No buddy, I need privacy by myself." He still didn't go out and replied (whilst opening the closet door) "I'm getting it Mommy" and hands me a tampon! He didn't know what it was for just that I needed 'privacy' to use it. I forget how much information he is actually absorbing!
Natalia, USA

I tried to explain the difference between boys and girls to my Son. He got it but then as he was proud of knowing he would tell everyone we met "I've got a willy but my Mummy hasn't got a willy." It can get quite embarrassing when he says it to people we don't know!
Holly, UK

I was sitting on the computer one evening and my children were watching cartoons before bed. When I looked over to check on them I saw my Son (aged four) playing with himself. I asked him what he was doing and his very animated response was, "Well my penis just popped up so I was trying to put it back down." I broke down in a hysterical laugh not quite knowing what to say to him! Ha Ha!
Janine, USA

I have a little girl who is almost three years old. I also have a friend who has a three month old little Boy. My friend came over to visit one day and as happens with babies, he needed a diaper change. So while my friend

was changing him, my little girl was watching intently and as soon as my friend goes to close the new diaper up my Daughter leaned down, pulled the diaper back, looked up at me and said "Mommy look! Him have a tail!"
My Friend and I were laughing for ages, but then I knew it was time to have the boy/girl talk!
Mya, USA

We went 'trick or treating' and I had to explain to my two boys that they were not allowed to eat any candy until we checked it. As they were walking back from a house my oldest (who was six) shouted at the top of his lungs "Mommy! Can you check this for poison?" The thirty plus people around couldn't stop laughing and the old Women at the house he had just left were not impressed! I'm not ashamed to say I was a little bit proud!
Leila, USA

I was playing outside with my four year old Daughter and she said, "I'm going to have a mean face someday".
I asked her "why?"
She said "Because I'm going to be a Mommy someday and Mommies have mean faces."
Alana, USA

My four year old had chicken, dumplings and peas for dinner. He came in the room I was in and said "Mommy I'm done."
I asked him "Did you eat all of it?"
He replied "Yes Mommy, I even ate the little green balls."

Laugh Out Loud! Kids

So funny!
Madison, USA

While potty training my now four year old Daughter we were having issues with her pooping. She would hold it for almost a week unless we gave her a laxative or an enema. One day we sat her on the potty and told her she needed to poop or we couldn't go to the zoo. After straining for a moment the movement happened. A big grin spread across her face and she shouted "Thank you, butt!"
Funniest moment of my life!
Jen, USA

I do remember my Niece (who was three at the time) when I was about eight months pregnant, we were sitting at a table in a restaurant, when she looked at me so seriously and asked "Why do you have a baby in your tummy?" I quickly answered that God had put it there for me. She thought about it for a minute and stuck out her hand, palm up and said "Okay, spit it out!" I laughed so hard I thought that I might have the baby right then and there! I guessed that she figured the only way to get things in your tummy was to swallow them so that must be the way that they come out too!
Kelsey, UK

We got a new kitten at the weekend. My son (he's three) was talking to it and it mewed at him. My son looked at me and said, "I think that's French for hello." Ha Ha!
Joanne, UK

My Daughter went into the garage to see what her Daddy was doing the other day. She came running into the house shouting "Mummy Mummy! Daddy's bike is doing a wee wee in the potty!" I went into the garage to see what she was talking about and Daddy was changing the oil on his motorbike! There was a little stream of oil coming out of the bottom of the bike into a bucket underneath! So cute!
Heather, UK

My five year old Son and I were talking about babies one day. He said "I'm going to have lots of babies."
I told him "You have to get married first."
He said "Eeww I'm not getting married, I'm just going to have babies. I'll live with you and let you take care of them!" Thanks Son!
Katie, USA

When one of my boys was three we went swimming with his female Cousin who was also three. In the changing room he gasped in horror and shouted at the top of his lungs "Mummy, her tiddler has fell off!" My sister and I cracked up, then had to explain the difference between boys and girls! Ha Ha!
Nicola, UK

I went to the Zoo with my children and when we got to the turtle enclosure, one of them was partially on top of the other. Of course I knew what was going on, but my

then eight year old Son looked at the enclosure and said "All that room and he couldn't go around?" Myself and other parents nearby were cracking up!
Hayley, UK

While at Disneyland for Christmas, we were meeting Mickey and Minnie at the same time. My almost three year old Son looked at Mickey, then at Minnie, and in front of a thousand people said, as serious as can be, "Mommy, Mickey has a penis, and Minnie has a vagina right?" My husband and I just looked at each other, laughed, and told him, "Yes, that's right." Oh the look on all those people's faces was priceless!
Jessica, USA

One day I was laying on my bed watching TV and my Son came in and sat down next to me. He didn't say anything at first, he just lifted up my shirt so he could see my belly. I went back to watching TV, assuming that he was going to blow raspberries on my stomach. When he just continued to sit there staring at my stomach, I asked what he was doing. He ran his hands across my belly and said, "I'm looking for the door." This obviously confused me, so I asked him, "What door?" He sighed and said, "You told me I grew in your belly. I'm looking for the door I came out of when I was born." I managed to keep a straight face long enough to tell him that there was no door, and that when he was older I'd explain to him how babies got out of Mommies' tummies. He left and I laughed so hard, I nearly wet myself.
Helen, USA

The funniest thing I ever remember a kid saying was said by my Nephew, who was about three at the time. He and my Husband were play wrestling on the ground. My Husband is very hairy and his shirt came up during the roughhousing. My Nephew stood back with wide eyes and said in an awed voice, "You have feathers!"
Victoria, USA

With it being winter I'm not worried about shaving my legs every day but I might change that after my two year old little boy ran his fingers over my legs (only two days growth at that point) and said "Ouch!" Very loudly! He now takes great delight in pulling my jeans leg up when we are in company and doing it again!
Jacqui, UK

I remember having a discussion about what happens when you die with my Daughter when she was about four. I said that some people thought that you go to Heaven, which is a lovely place where everyone is kind. I had started to run out of things to say by then so finished it off with "… and everyone sits on lovely soft clouds." When we'd finished talking about it she said "When I go to Heaven I want to sit on a chair." Ha Ha!
Jamie, USA

We were having lunch in a café, and I asked my youngest Daughter if she wanted to try for a 'wee wee' before we left (she is two and a half).

"Nope!" She said "I don't have any water in my bum."
Tina, UK

Whilst sat in a very nice restaurant one evening, we were in mid conversation and something funny was said so I was laughing and my little girl turned to me and shouted "Mummy Mummy! Your boobies are dancing!" The next day I went and got fitted for a better bra!
Cerys, UK

My Daughter said today that they have been learning about London at school so I asked her a few questions about what she had learned.
I asked "Who lives in London?"
She said "The Queen and Prince William and his Wife."
"Good" I said, "Does anyone else live in London that you may know?"
She said "Yes, David Cameron."
"What does David Cameron do for a job?"
She said "He's the Prime Minister and at the weekends he's called Simon Cowell and appears on the X-Factor." Ha Ha! I don't know where she got that from!
Nicole, UK

Around the time of potty training I was constantly asking my Daughter "Do you need a wee?" She must have got fed up with me asking as she sighed, tutted and said "No Mummy! My wee wee's not all filled up again yet!"
Teagan, UK

I loved Christmas this year with my three year old. The look on his face was priceless when he saw his massive pile of gifts. He then turned round and saw a smaller pile on the couch and asked who they were for. "They're mine darling." I said to which he replied
"Wow Mum, you must have been naughty!" Ha Ha!
Hayley, UK

My Son asked lots of questions about my late Dad and what happened to him after he died. As soon as I was able to, I took him to the garden of remembrance where my Dad's ashes are. My Son looked at the small plaque for a while and turned to me and asked "Was he really that small?" He really cheered me up, bless him!
Corrine, UK

This was a conversation I had with my four year old Daughter one day:-
Daughter: "My best friends have willy's." (Her two best friends are boys)
Me: "That's right darling."
Daughter: "Has Daddy got a willy?"
Me: "Yes darling, you know he has, he's a boy too."
Daughter: "Oh it looked like a snake in the bath."
So funny! I didn't tell my Husband, his ego is big enough as it is!
Louisa, UK

Our little girl will frequently go up to me or her Dad and say "You know when I was a little boy..." We keep

Laugh Out Loud! Kids

explaining that she has *always* been a girl!
Pauline, UK

When my oldest Daughter was around two years old, her Dad was having a shower and she wandered into the bathroom whilst I was in the bedroom. She came running back out shouting "Mummy come quick! Daddy's got a poo coming out his front bum!" Her Dad was mortified whilst I was in stitches!
Cathy, UK

Once when my Niece (four years old) and my Son (three years old) took a bath together for the first time, they were happily playing in the tub with toys until suddenly my son yelled, "Mommy come quick!" (I was in the hallway folding towels watching them, but he couldn't see me) and I asked "What's the matter?"
He replied, pointing in horror at his Cousin "Her ding ding fell off and we have to find it before it goes down the pipes!" That prompted the discussion of the physical difference between girls and boys! Ha Ha!
Susie, UK

We were at the park with my six year old Niece when this little boy, about her age, walked up to her and asked "Do you want to date me?"
My Niece said "Uh, no only if I wanted a baby or something, which I don't."
Where did that come from?
Faye, USA

When my son was seven years old, I was headed to the grocery store and he came along. As we were pulling out of the neighborhood, he noticed I wasn't wearing my wedding ring and asked why. I told him that my hands had been swollen the night before and I forgot to put it back on. He was a bit upset and wanted me to go back home and get it. I told him that I wasn't turning around, just to get the ring. Then he said the most adorable, sweetest thing ever, "But Mom, if you're not wearing your ring, someone else will steal you!"
Aww!
Mandy, USA

My three year old Daughter was standing outside with my Mom and my neighbor, chatting away. My Daughter was playing happily in the grass when my neighbor's girlfriend asked for a corkscrew to open her wine bottle. I told her that I actually don't drink wine so I don't own a corkscrew. My Daughter promptly speaks up and says "My Gramma gots one cause she's a wino!" Dear me, where do they come up with this stuff? I certainly never said it to her!
Elizabeth, USA

Cute and Random Comments and Actions:-

Sometimes our kids just come out with something completely out of the blue. These random comments can have us giggling so much more because they are so unexpected
They can be funny, embarrassing or cheeky but sometimes they say something so sweet we are putty in their hands for a while.

The other day my friend offered my little girl some sweets and she said, in the most serious and grown up 'old lady' voice "No thank you, I don't really eat those these days!"
Georgia, USA

My Son makes me laugh with all the random stuff he comes out with. A week ago I asked him what he wanted to eat and he screamed "Toothpaste butty!"
Then the other day I was changing his dirty nappy, when I was done he saw it open on the floor and went "Ooh look, cake!"
Jennifer, UK

My Daughter is hilarious at the moment as she is calling everyone and everything "Darling". We walked past a group of teenage boys earlier and she patted one of them on the leg and said "Love you darling." The boys cracked up laughing at her, of all the things she could have said to them, they didn't expect that!
Kate, UK

One night I went to tuck my Daughter into bed and she woke up, opened her eyes and asked "Is Daddy tayto?" (Is daddy a potato?") I laughed so hard!
Rachel, UK

While my Daughter was sitting on my Hubby's knee, facing him, I was asking "where's Daddy's nose? Where's Daddy's chin?" etc. Then I asked her "Where's Daddy's hair?" He has a shaved head and she looked at him for a few seconds, with a confused look on her face before rubbing his head and going "Oh dear, no hair!" So Funny!
Deborah, UK

If my Daughter drops something or falls over, she can be heard saying "It's ok, it's my fault." I can't help but laugh at how sweet that is!
Melanie, UK

A couple of days ago, my Son was in the loo and I went to check everything was okay. He was standing with his pants around his ankles, but there was a big puddle on

the floor. I asked what happened. He said, "Well, I was pulling my pants down and I heard a funny noise. I looked down, and my willy was doing a wee - all by itself!" I almost wet myself it was so funny!
Angie, UK

A conversation between my toddler and me the other day:
Me: "Sweetie, what does a cat say?"
Him: "Meeeoooow."
Me: "What does a dog say?"
Him: "Woof woof woof."
Me: "What does a duck say?"
Him: "Quack quack."
Me: "What does Mummy say?"
Him: "No, No, No!"
Ha Ha! Thanks Son!
Moira, UK

We are currently in the middle of teaching our Son to use his manners and he is doing really well. He has a toy kitchen which has an ice dispenser on the fridge which will shoot out plastic ice cubes when you turn the knob. Well every time he turned the knob and an ice cube came out he would say to the ice cube "Thank you." Afterwards, he came out of his bedroom, moved his shoes out of the way and said "Scuse me".
I was giggling away, listening to him!
Amy, UK

My Friend had brought her Daughter round for a play

date with my Daughter and they were both playing together in our garden. After a while they came into the kitchen and my Daughter said "We both have to go potty but we're going to hold it our whole life. Then we'll go in the cemetery."
My Friend's Daughter then added "Yeah, we'll pee when we're dead!"
My Friend and I laughed, but then told them that they really ought to come in and go before they had an accident!
Casey, USA

Today at the park my little boy was trying to talk to a boy on the swings, so he started with "Excuse me" which got no response, then louder "Excuse me!" and finally "EXCUSE ME DARLING!" Then when we were walking home he said "I need to go to sleep" so I said "Okay," to which he responded "I can't. There's no bed here."
He makes me laugh all the time, his logic is amazing!
Natalie, UK

My Daughter made my whole family laugh today when she was at my Mum's for Sunday lunch. She was rationing her cuddles and she said "I don't want run out of cuddles for you all."
Kelly, UK

My Niece just stopped when we were walking to the shop about a month ago. I asked "What's the matter?"
She said "I've runned out of walk."

Ha Ha! It was very funny and cute!
Tara, USA

I told my Son that I love him more than cake.
Of his own accord he replied, "I love you more than chicken nuggets Mummy."
Samantha, UK

A few weeks ago we had the guy over to fix our satellite dish and re-program our TV's. He seemed to be here forever working on it. My Husband arrived home and my Son saw him at the window. He ran up to me and said "Daddy's home, Daddy's gonna see that guy in Mommy's room. Hide that guy!"
Then when my Husband came in, my Son grabbed him by the hand and took him to our bedroom and said "Look at that guy." Ha Ha!
Jamie, USA

My Son was sat at the window thinking and then said "Mummy, I'm very clever aren't I? I think I must be God!"
Janine, UK

A few days ago My Son and I made brownies with chocolate icing and of course he was eating as well as 'helping'. He had a bit around his mouth and he looked at me and used his finger to circle around his mouth and said "I'm gonna save this for later." I almost peed myself laughing!
Helen, UK

When we were at my Mother In Law's last week my Mother In Law was walking around looking for her broom. She asked my Son if he had seen it and he told her "Maybe the witch took it."
Jenna, USA

I was out shopping with my Son a while ago and he was misbehaving in the store (terrible two's!) and I had been asking him to be good. He spotted something he wanted and asked "Mommy, can I have a toy?"
I said "No, not until you are being a good boy." I had to stop myself from laughing when he stopped to think and then answered "But I is good, now."
Hannah, USA

My Son and I were sitting with the patio doors open as it was a nice day. We heard a low flying helicopter so we both ran outside and he starts waving and bless his little heart, shouted "It's an emergency! Oh no!" It was so cute!
Melissa, UK

I was listening to my Son talking to himself one day and overheard him stop chatting and start crying, I was about to go and find out what was wrong when I heard him telling himself "Don't cry!" Then he continued chatting to himself.
Joanie, USA

At soft play this morning my Son told another little boy "Be careful cos she's just a baby," pointing at a little one year old girl. Then he was asking the little girl "Are you fine?" She was following him everywhere, it was so cute!
Gillian, UK

My Daughter farted in the car yesterday and said, "That was my bottom. Not Mummy's bottom or Grandma's bottom." Then a lorry went past us and she said "Not lorry's bottom."
Kelly, UK

I took my little boy to have lunch with my Mum today, she works at the hospital.
We were walking along the corridor and he just started saying "Hello" to everyone who walked past him followed by "Bye bye." Thankfully most people said "Hello" back to him but if someone didn't he kept saying "Oh no, no bye bye" bless him, it made me giggle.
Alison, UK

When my youngest Daughter was three I will never forget the day she was walking funny, and when I asked her why she said "Mummy, my bum has eaten my knickers."
Karla, UK

When my Son was nearly three and potty training we had family round and he escaped to the bathroom to use the potty. After a few minutes he returned to the living room with his trousers around his ankles shouting "Mummy!

There's a rainbow in my willy!" It turned out he had just found a vein! That's definitely one I will be reminding him of when he's older!
Michelle, UK

My Son's favourite pastime at the moment is doing impressions of pigeons walking! "They go like this..." He says whilst waddling along!
Natalie, UK

My six year old was given a glow in the dark onesie for his birthday. He went to bed fine, but then twenty minutes later he came downstairs to inform me "When I glow in the dark I scare myself." He decided he would rather not sleep in it after that!
Amanda, UK

My Daughter is always coming out with such random comments. Last week she announced (out of the blue) that she wasn't going to wax her legs when she was older, she was simply going to comb them and make the hair nice and curly - she's only four and a half years old!
Sophie, UK

We were out for a Christmas meal at a restaurant and the waiter was chatting to my Son. He asked him "Have you seen our Christmas tree?"
He replied, with a confused tone, "Is it lost?"
Nicole, USA

My Hubby was in the loo this afternoon and my three and a half year old little boy knocked on the door and asked very loudly, "Daddy are you picking your nose? Cos if you do, you will get carrots."
I haven't a clue where he's got that one from ha ha!
Ruby, UK

This one was really sweet, I was really tired one morning and struggling to wake up properly, and my little one was in bed with me. He looked at me and said "Mummy, it's okay, you can have your dream back now."
Jess, UK

My little boy is so funny that the Nursery Teacher has said he should have his own TV show! He is only four but when one of the other children was playing up at Nursery he actually said to the Nursery Nurse, "You think they would know better now they are four wouldn't you?" Ha Ha!
Jane, UK

We went shopping earlier and my one year old Son walked around pointing to his bum going "My bum, my bum" all the way around the shop. Just the way he says it makes me laugh!
Emma, UK

My Son is twenty one months and keeps saying "Deal or no deal?" If I ask him to do something, he'll often answer with "No deal."
Susan, UK

My six year old wanted a toy from a store while we were out one day. We decided he could have it as he had been good and with the biggest smile ever and so excited, he said "I've wanted this my whole life!" He had everyone in the store laughing - His entire six years of life!
Jenny, USA

My two year old stuck a sanitary pad to each of her hands and came running out of the bathroom yelling "I'm a crab!"
Clare, UK

One windy day my four year old was riding his bike. We were on our way back from the park. I told him that it was really windy and he said "Yeah my nuts are freezing!"
I couldn't believe he said that. I laughed so hard!
Tina, UK

I have a three year old Son and he really loves chocolate milk. We were driving home from my Sister's house and my Son was sitting in the back seat when he tells me "Mom, my balls hurt cos they need chocolate milk." I was in complete shock and didn't know what to say!
Marley, USA

Laugh Out Loud! Kids

I was shopping with my six year old son and he yelled out "Hey Mom! Look at the fat chick!" I turned around in horror expecting to see the Woman he was insulting, only to see him smiling and holding up a big fluffy yellow chicken!
Ellie, USA

My five year old asked me the other day, "Have you ever seen an Elephant in a Cherry Tree?"
"No" I replied
She said "They're good hiders aren't they?"
Where do they get this stuff from?
Christy, USA

My Daughter was about three and we always put talc on her after her bath. Well this particular night she decided to take care of it herself, and I do mean she took care of it. She was totally covered from her neck down to her feet with baby powder. I walked in and she's looking at me saying "Look Mom, I put some powder on" with this great big smile on her face. All I could do was laugh, and love her just a little bit more!
Jo, USA

My Son was two at the time and playing with his cars. A bunch of them fell on the floor and he said "Oh my goodness, my cars fall down" in the most serious voice you could possibly imagine. Ha Ha! He makes me laugh on a daily basis with some of the things that come out of his

mouth.
Rita, USA

A couple of weeks ago, My Son came running down the hallway with a saucer-sled in front of him as a shield. Then he turned around and I realized he had toilet paper tucked in his shorts. He was being Captain America and wanted to have a cape!
Unfortunately, the toilet paper was still attached to the roll. So I had 40ft of toilet paper to clean up. Also when he breaks something or knocks it over, he tells me "I didn't mean to do it, my brain told me to!"
Tracy, USA

Yesterday I asked my six year old to get me my purse. He went and got it, and then kinda strutted around with it. I went to grab it off of him and he said (as sassy as can be) "Don't you be grabbin my Man purse!" I almost fell over laughing!
Cindy, USA

The other day I took my three year old Son skiing. At the end of the lesson I was changing him from his long underwear (with briefs underneath) to his jeans. As he was in nothing but his underpants he turned to an old lady sitting at the table next to us, and screamed at the top of his lungs "Don't look at my penis!" The lady looked mortified but I just thought it was hilarious!
Marcy, USA

Today at breakfast, my three year old Son was eating apples and decided to joke around and told us he was eating bananas. We laughed with him, then he made us belly laugh with his follow-up comment "I crack myself up!"
Leona, USA

I was making a stir-fry with my Daughter who is nearly three. She likes to help, and after chopping up the zucchini she put it in the bowl. I turned around and she was holding two of the round slices up over her little nipples and said "Mummy, look, nipples!" I laugh every time I cook with zucchini now.
Megan, USA

When my youngest was three, we were riding in the car and she was trying to talk and my other two children were talking over her. She Shoved her hand up in the air and said "Excuse me, I'm talking here!" It was so funny, but it worked - the other two stopped talking!
Tia, USA

My Daughter had a little tea set and it was one of her favourite toys. My Husband was in the living room engrossed in the evening news when she brought him a little cup of 'tea', which was just water. After several cups of tea and lots of praise for such yummy tea, I came home. My Husband made me wait in the living room to watch her bring him a cup of tea, because it was 'just the cutest thing!' I waited, and sure enough, here she came down the hall with a cup of tea for Daddy and I watched

him drink it up.
Then I said, (as only a mother would know) "Did it ever occur to you that the only place she can reach to get water is the toilet?" He went a shade of red I hadn't seen before and looked like he was going to be sick! I just couldn't believe he hadn't wondered where it was coming from!
Becky, UK

My Daughter has been telling everyone who comes to our house that there is bird poo on the window (she is fixated on it) and tells them very seriously that "It isn't tasty." I have no idea if she has just decided it isn't or has actually eaten some (yuck!).
Catherine, UK

I asked my Son today "What are you eating?" As he seemed to be chewing something. His reply was a delighted "Bogies!"
Natasha, UK

My four year old and I had a conversation about boogers one day (as you do). He kept saying the word so I decided to find out if he actually knew what they were. I asked him "What is a booger?"
He said "A booger is a stinky bug that lives in your nose, then you put it on your finger and hang it on the wall - and it's crunchy."
"How do you know it's crunchy?" My Husband asked him.

My Son said "It gets crunchy when you wear it in your nose a long time." Ha Ha! He obviously knew a lot more than I thought!
Maria, USA

I was out walking with my four year old Son one day and we saw a dead bird. He pointed at it and said "Oh dear." I tried to tell a little white lie (so it wouldn't upset him) so I said "It's okay, it's just some fluff."
He gave a big sigh and said "Mum, it's a dead bird. It's okay, don't worry" and patted my arm. It was so sweet!
Nicola, UK

When it was snowing my eldest who is five kept slipping in the snow. After falling at least a dozen times he got up and said "Mum why does it always happen to me?"
Another day he just wouldn't stop messing around. I told him off and he said "It's not my fault Mum, I keep telling my brain to stop messing about but it just doesn't listen." I couldn't help but laugh!
Sammie, UK

My little girl was asking me for a story at bedtime one night. She kept asking for a story from my mouth. I didn't understand what she meant so asked her to explain and she said "I don't want one from a book, from your mouth Mummy." I realised she meant she wanted me to make one up!
Natasha, UK

My Son was sat on the toilet one day where he frequently starts really random and funny conversations. This particular day he was talking about his little friend who lived down the street and was the same age as him (three). "He has the same bottom as me and Daddy, doesn't he? With a little snail coming out of it."
I was really trying not to giggle and said "Really, does he?"
My Son nodded and said, very seriously "Yes, only his is a tiny little snail and Daddy's is a big snail"
I tried not to laugh my head off and replied "That's nice to know, Son."
He replied "That's okay Mummy, I've finished now, you can wipe my bum."
I told his friend's Mum the next day although I found it difficult as I was laughing so much!
Hannah, UK

My Son was four years old and he shouted me from his room. I went to him and was shocked to find him naked and was wiggling his hips! I asked him what he was doing and he said "Look Mummy, my willy's waving at you!"
I had to then keep a straight face and explain to him that he couldn't do it when he was at playgroup etc!
Maria, UK

My three year old Son said the other day "Mum, I love you" which I found really sweet.
I said "I love you too honey."
He replied with "Do you want my bogey?" The way he looked at me, he obviously thought this was a lovely gift but I said "Erm, no honey, you put it in a tissue, it isn't

nice to give bogies to people." He looked a bit confused but then ran off and carried on playing, Yuck!
Gemma, UK

I work at a Pre-school and we had a work experience girl with us this one week. One little Girl took a shine to her and was asking her lots of questions. I overheard her ask "Do have any Children?"
The work experience girl replied "No, not yet."
The little girl looked at her sympathetically and said "Never mind, maybe next week."
Ha Ha!
Beth, UK

I was sitting on the sofa watching a film with my four year old Daughter.
She said "Mummy."
"Yes sweetie?" I asked
"I like your armpits better then Daddy's."
"Why is that?" I asked (trying not to laugh).
"Cos Daddy's are too fluffy and yours are nice."
"Oh, that's nice." I said, I really didn't know what else to say to that!
Caroline, UK

My eldest Daughter, when she was about three years old told me "I want to have boobies Mummy, but I don't want those pointy bits on the end." I had to point out she already had those bits - bless her.

Another time she was sat on the toilet doing 'air writing'

and asking me to give her words for her to spell. She was writing across in front of herself and when she reached the wall she went back and rubbed it all out as she'd run out of room! Their imagination is amazing!
Laura, UK

My Son was around three and a half and was on the phone to his Nanna. He told her that his willy had died and he was scared it was going to drop off!
Julie, UK

One evening my Daughter wanted to go to the toilet. She had only been in bed for an hour or so but was obviously in a deep sleep and hadn't fully woken up. I took her to the toilet and she was falling asleep on the toilet and then all of a sudden she said " Mummy my poo poo won't come out as its too busy reading a book" I was in hysterics laughing and the next morning I asked her about it and she just looked at me as if I was crazy! She obviously didn't remember.
Lucy, UK

My four year old Niece was on the toilet at my house once and screamed "Auntie I can't go!" I asked her "Why?"
She said "It's holding on for dear life!" I couldn't answer her as I was laughing too much!
Toni, UK

I once told my Daughter and Son "You can have one thing from the shops."
My Daughter came back with some chocolate, but my Son (aged three at the time) staggered down the aisle carrying this huge joint of ham, saying very seriously "I'll have this Mum." I was speechless for a while!
Trina, UK

I was visiting my Sister and her kids for the holidays and they made me laugh the whole time I was there, especially my younger Niece.
My four year old Niece was coloring on the floor as her cupcakes were baking in the oven. She stuck her nose up in the air, sniffed and said "It smells like cake in my nose!" Later on we went to the pool and her older Sister was playing with some older kids. The four year old threw some rings in the pool but before she could jump in, the other kids got them all. She screamed at them, "You cheaters! I'm supposed to win!"

My husband and I took both girls horseback riding. The four year old asked, "Why does it smell like poop in here? Don't those ponies know how to flush?"

We went to watch fireworks and the girls were running around trying to get me to chase them. The four year old said, "Bet you can't catch me! Mommy can't catch me and you have legs just like her!"

I asked them if they missed their baby Brother and the four year old said, "No, he cries too much. Nobody likes a cry baby."
Jordyn, USA

My three year old Son once told me when I was pregnant with his baby Brother "I have a baby too, mine is in my leg."
Jennifer, USA

I was in the waiting room at the Doctors and reading my two year old Son 'Hansel and Gretel' and we were chatting about the pictures etc. We got to the page where the scary old witch is luring them inside. He points to her and yells "Gramma!" I couldn't stop laughing! The people in the Doctor's office thought it was quite humorous too.
Abby, USA

Inquisitive Kids and Questions:-

We all know that kids like to ask questions, until I had my own I really had no idea that they never stop asking questions until they go to sleep! Old questions, new questions, mainly the same questions over and over again! They are naturally inquisitive which helps them learn, but can be really funny too.

The other day, we were all playing in the garden when I noticed something had been strewn all over the lawn by the hedge. I went to have a look, and realised it was a box of Tampons. Several had been taken out of the box and out of the wrappers, and then discarded. I asked my Son who was almost three if he knew anything about it.
He frowned. "Yes" he said, "They're not sweeties!"
Tracy, UK

My Niece is five years old. She was singing the alternative Happy Birthday song at the weekend (you know 'you look like a monkey and you smell like one too'). She asked

"Mummy, what does 'one too' smell like?" Ha Ha!

Keira, UK

I overheard this conversation between my Son and my Mum the other day:
Son: "Grandma, when you were my age, were there Dinosaurs?"
Mum: (Unimpressed!) "No."
Son: "Oh. Well, did you live in a cave then?"
Ha Ha!
Janine, UK

I was at my Friend's house one day and her four year old had gone quiet in the kitchen so her Mum went to check on her. She had a bottle of children's chewable vitamins in her hands and was trying to open the 'sweeties.' My friend said "They aren't sweeties, and you can only have one a day. You can't open them because the bottle is child proof." Her Daughter had us both in stitches when she looked up, amazed and asked "How does it know it's me?"
Stella, UK

My Son and I were walking through the park one day when we walked past a young couple kissing. My Son was very interested in them and watched the whole time we were near them. When they were out of sight he turned to me and asked "Why is he whispering in her mouth?"
Jess, UK

My Daughter really embarrassed me the other day at the supermarket. An elderly Lady I know was there and stopped to speak to me. My Daughter was staring at her intently and I could just tell she was going to say something. I dreaded what it was but even I was surprised when she asked her "Why doesn't your skin fit your face?"
I was mortified and apologised to the Lady and made a quick exit!
Layla, UK

I remember my eldest Daughter asking me once (when she was around four years old) "Mummy, when Nan was a little girl and the world was black and white, did they have TV's?"
I was glad Nan wasn't there when she asked!
Joanne, UK

My little boy was at the age where he was constantly asking questions. He was sitting watching 'Tom and Jerry' this one particular day and asked "Where do Tom and Jerry go when the commercials are on?"
I couldn't think of an answer so I changed the subject!
Anna, USA

We lived in Dundee when we were younger, which is built on the plug of an extinct volcano. One day my little Brother asked my Mum "Mum? What did you do when the volcano erupted?"
She explained that despite what he thought she wasn't

that old!
Gemma, UK

My Daughter is always coming out with funny comments which are sometimes completely random, like the time she asked "Mummy, do cats have eyebrows?"
Emma, UK

We went on holiday with my Parents a few Years ago and my Son was with my Mum when she was getting changed for dinner. When she took her clothes off to put her dress on, he was stood watching her. She asked him what was wrong, and he asked her "Does Granddad laugh at you when you take your clothes off?"
Good job she has a sense of humour!
Gillian, UK

When my Daughter was two, we were in the bath one night, when she asked "Mummy why do you have a hairy minky? Can I stroke it?" She seemed upset when I said "No we don't do that."
Melissa, UK

My Daughter was about seven and asked me one day "Mum, what animals do sausages come from?"
"They usually come from pigs" I said.
About five minutes later, after thinking about it, she asked "Mum, do pigs poo sausages?"
Lorna, UK

When we were discussing our family tree at home my Dad mentioned that his Parents were dead. My Son (aged four) thought very hard and then asked "Were they killed by pirates?"
Alison, USA

Me and my Daughter, aged three, were snuggled on the sofa, talking. She asked me "Why do I have a Mummy and Daddy?" I told her "Because we love each other very much and made you."
She thought about it and then asked "With Selotape?"
Michelle, UK

I was at my Mum's one summer when my Nephews were playing in her new hot tub. I was sitting on the side when the youngest asked me "Did you play in here when you were a little boy?"
Helen, UK

My three year old Son asked me the other day where my 'winky' was. I explained that I was a girl and so I didn't have one. He then asked "Why? Did you touch it too much and make it fall off?"
Jenna, UK

My Granddaughter had been learning a little about reproduction and had gotten confused. She asked "If I was made from an egg and a tadpole, where did the

eggshell go?"
Margaret, UK

We needed a new shower curtain, and we had my three year old son pick out the new one. He chose one with dolphins in the ocean on it. So the next day, I asked him if he wanted to shower first with the new curtain and he was excited until we got into the bathroom, then he said, "No, I don't want to." So, I jumped in for my shower and he asked "Are there sharks in there?"
Martina, USA

While in deep thought in the back seat of the car my Son asked "Mom, if Adam and Eve are the first two people God made then what number am I? Number twenty or something?"
Ha Ha! I explained there were a lot more people in the world than that!
Andrea, USA

The other day we went to my Cousin's house and their six year old looked at our five month old Son with a puzzled look on his face. He then asked (very seriously) "Who shaved his head?"
Christa, USA

My eight year old asked me the other day "Why do people listen to IPods? Why don't they just listen to the songs in their heads?"
Carly, UK

We were out driving a few days ago and my three year old Son asked us (in a very serious voice) "Where do the farts go?" He really wanted to know but we couldn't stop laughing, it was so cute!
Belinda, USA

The other day I sat down to play with my almost five year old Daughter. She told me she wanted us to do a puzzle together. I started to put the pieces together and she was just watching me. I asked if she was going to help and she said "No, I am the supervisor."
What a cheeky monkey!
Isla, USA

I was walking to School one morning with my six year old and on our route we pass a Funeral Home. On this occasion a coffin was being brought out to the hearse and of course she wanted to know what was in 'the box'. I explained that it was someone who had died and she started freaking out. I managed to calm her down and when she asked "Mummy, do they bury *all* bodies?" After the way she had reacted when I told her what was in the coffin I decided to leave the subject of cremation for another day so just told her I thought they did. She trotted off into school quite happily but full of questions. Come home time she came out of School and shouted to me from the door "Mummy! Why didn't you tell me they burn bodies?" I got some very strange looks as the Teacher explained to me that she had discussed

cremation with her!
Holly, UK

I was talking to my new boss while my Son was with me. I hadn't noticed that he had got into my bag but he started to tap me on the leg and asked "Mummy, can I have this sweetie?" I looked down and he was holding up a tampon in its wrapper. I went bright red whilst explaining that it wasn't a 'sweetie.' It broke the ice though as my boss found it very funny!
Maddie, UK

When my Son was four he was obsessed with dinosaurs. He talked about them quite a lot and would always ask, "What if they come eat us?" I would always tell him that they can't as they are all dead. Occasionally we would drive by the Cemetery and he would ask what it was, so I would tell him that it was where people who died were buried. One day we drove past a Cemetery, and he asked if the dinosaurs were buried there. I said "Yes."
My son asked "Can they see if they are buried?"
"No" I said.
He thought about it for a minute and then asked "Why not? Did somebody poke their eyes out?" I was in tears laughing so hard, because I was trying to explain death and burial to a four year old and it was just creating more questions!
Charlotte, USA

One day we were in the car with my Husband driving and I was holding two cups of coffee. Our Daughter (aged two at the time) said "Mommy! Give me five."
I said "I can't honey. I don't have any hands." Our Daughter thought I said I didn't have any pants and asked "Why not?" I jokingly told her (still thinking we are talking about hands), "Daddy must have taken them off".
Our Daughter asked "Why did Daddy take your pants off in the car?" It's a good job no one was listening to our conversation!
Abbie, USA

Honesty:-

Honesty can be good, we want our kids to tell the truth don't we? Well actually no, *sometimes* we would prefer it if they weren't quite so honest!

One day I was babysitting my three year old Cousin and I asked him "Do you want to watch Spongebob Squarepants?"
He said "No, that's lame, I want to watch a shark kill something."
Joanna, USA

I work in a Pre-school and one of the Children came up to me and said "My Mom's Auntie died at the weekend."
I said "Oh no, that's terrible. Is she ok?" (meaning was her Mom Ok)
"No" she said, with the most serious expression "She's dead."
Alyssa, USA

Laugh Out Loud! Kids

My younger Brother is autistic and thinks rather literally. After a long lecture on how to stand in line properly, the Teacher asked him, "Where are your hands?" She was hoping for his answer to be "To myself" but couldn't handle it when he threw up his hands and shouted, "At the end of my arms! Where else would they be?"
We had to explain to her that he wasn't being cheeky, he was just answering her question.
Amy, USA

I have a big family and my Nieces crack me up constantly when I see them.
My sister had a baby two months ago and my three year old Niece asked her "When is that baby gonna come out?"
My Sister replied "He's here look, he was in my tummy but he came out" to which my Niece replied "Oh I know, he's just so awful!"
I nearly peed myself!
Charlotte, USA

My Daughter is brutally honest and it can be worrying as you just don't know what she is going to say to people. The other day she told my Mum "You can't sit on that chair because your bum is too big to fit." I wanted the ground to swallow me up when she said that!
Katie, UK

One day my Daughter said "Mummy, if you get rid of your fat, make your hair nice, put some make up and nice

clothes on, you could go on 'Dancing on Ice!"
"Thanks for that sweetie" I said, Ha Ha!
Sam, UK

My Niece was round at our house once when my friend was. My friend turned to her and gave her a really cheesy, silly grin. She never skipped a beat, shouting "Your teeth are really yellow!" I almost died trying not to laugh! Another time she couldn't find her trainers and another friend asked her "Where were your trainers when you last saw them?" She replied "On my feet of course!"
Emma, UK

I was once trying on a red swimming costume at home, when my Son, who was then four, came walking in. He stood and looked at me then said "Oh Mummy you look just beautiful." I was just thinking how sweet that was when he added (smiling sweetly) "You look just like a big red ball." Needless to say, the swimming costume was returned to the shop.
Becky, UK

My Son wanted to take a picture of his Nanna but Nanna refused, saying "I don't like having my picture taken." My Son then looked very sad, thought about it and then asked her "Is that because you've got a spotty face, and a wrinkly neck?" Nanna wasn't impressed!
Rachel, UK

Laugh Out Loud! Kids

I remember when I was little a Man used to come to the house when my Parents were arranging a mortgage or Insurance (I was too young to understand at the time). One Day in particular he was supposed to arrive but was late and I overheard my Mum asking my Dad "Where is that prat?" Well me being a typical child, I went with my Mum to answer the door when he eventually arrived and greeted him loudly with "Hello, my Mum thinks you're a prat." Oops!
Jenna, UK

I had just got out of the bath one day with a towel wrapped around me and my hair all frizzy when my Son came into the bathroom and said "Oh Mummy, you're very beautiful - even with scarecrow hair."
"Thanks love" I said (trying not to laugh!)
Lindsey, UK

My Son has been watching 'March of the Penguins' a lot recently and he is a little obsessed with Penguins now. I put him to bed last night and said "I love you" as I usually do. He usually says it back however this time he said (very seriously) "I like you Mummy, but I really love penguins."
Carol, UK

Whilst reading a story to my Daughter the other night we got talking about cows and sheep as they were in the story we were reading. I asked her what cows eat and she replied "Baked beans Mummy."
I asked her "Do you like baked beans?"

She replied "No Mummy, I like money."
I don't know where that came from!
Ella, UK

I was cuddling my Daughter to sleep the other day as she wasn't very well and I told my Son to wake me up if I fell asleep as I could feel myself getting very tired. Sure enough I did fall asleep so when I woke, I asked him why he didn't wake me (in a nice way). He said "Cause you never let me eat sweets when you're awake."
I asked him "How many sweets have you eaten?"
He said "Ten." I then went and put the sweets out of reach so he couldn't eat any more and he said "I can just stand on a chair and get them so I can still eat them. Are you going back to sleep yet Mummy?"
I then moved the sweets to a cupboard he couldn't reach (even with a chair) and after watching me do this my Son said "It doesn't matter, Daddy can get them for me when he gets home."
What a little monkey!
Jane, UK

My Son was sat on my bed the other night having a story while my Husband was in the shower. We heard the shower come on and my Son says completely seriously and innocently "Daddy is having a shower Mummy, and probably a poo as well."
I couldn't stop laughing! Mostly because it was true!
Charlene, UK

Laugh Out Loud! Kids

A few days ago while having Sunday dinner at my Parents' my four year old Son was listening to a conversation between my Parents about feeding table scraps to the dog. My Mom said "Don't give the fat to her, it'll make her sick."
"Why?" Asked my Son.
"Because fat is not healthy." She Said.
"My Mommy is fat he replied." I was sitting next to him and trying not to laugh when I said "Gee thanks sweetie." Then he looked up at me with a proud smile and said "You're Welcome."
Anna, USA

My Daughter is almost three and is a real little Madam. We were sat on the couch the other day together and she was looking so intensely at me when out came "Mummy, you have a really big nose!"
Oh the honesty - I don't think it *is* that big! Ha Ha!
Dawn, UK

My Daughter was going to stay the night with my Friend. I put her in her car and when I was walking away, I heard her tell my friend "Don't run over Mommy."
My friend asked "Why not?"
My Daughter said "Because sometimes my Daddy has to work late and I'm not allowed to stay at home by myself."
We laughed at that the next day!
Julia, USA

My Daughter's class had just had their photographs taken separately and then had a group shot as well. The

Teacher was trying to get the Parents to buy a copy of the group picture and was saying (to the Children) "Just think how nice it will be to look at it when you are all grown up and say, "There's Jennifer, she's a Lawyer" or "That's Michael, He's a Doctor." One of the Children then joined in very enthusiastically with "And there's the Teacher, she's dead."
The Teacher didn't answer, Ha Ha!
Krista, USA

My three year old comes out with all sorts. He said one day "I'm hungry because I haven't ate in five million years!"

Another time he wanted to go out with his Dad and I asked him "Why don't you want to stay with me?"
He answered "Sometimes I just need a break from you!"
"Ok" I said – Isn't that something I should say about him? Ha Ha!
Christina, USA

Yesterday was my Husband's birthday and with two kids we never get a date night but we had convinced my Mother In Law to keep the boys. She told us when we got home that when she had got our four year old out of the bathtub he farted. She said he looked at her and said "Granny, I promise I didn't do that, sometimes my butt makes mistakes."
So funny!
Maria, USA

The other day, while making my Daughter's bed I found a lovely picture of her as a baby in her Dad's arms, she was a newborn and had just come out of the ICU. I asked her "Why do you have the picture under your pillow?"
"Mum," She said "It makes me feel really safe and gives me good dreams and it reminds me of when Daddy used to be nice."
Ha Ha!
Amy, UK

I was standing in a queue in a clothes shop when my Daughter walked over with a very skimpy top. She held it up to me and said "This is nice Mummy."
"I think that's a bit small for Mummy, darling" I said.
She looked confused and said "But Mummy you've got no boobies."
"Thank You darling" was all I could manage in reply!
Jackie, UK

On the first day of school, most of the Parents follow the buses taking their kids to school and take pictures of them with their friends. My Son, who was in first grade told me he didn't want me to do that. I asked him why and he responded "Last year in kindergarten, I told the people in my class my Mom was pretty. I don't want them to know I lied."
Gee, thanks! Ha Ha!
Josie, USA

On a busy night, I put a can of spaghetti in the microwave

and put it in front of my kids. They told me "That's the best meal you've ever made us!"
I didn't think my cooking was that bad!
Trina, USA

To pass the time while on an airplane, my Son and I played 'I spy.' We took turns and on his turn he said "I spy something yellow." After many guesses, I gave up. He said "Mom! It's your teeth!"
Jen, USA

A few years ago, before bedtime, I offered to tell a story to my five year old and three year old. They asked me to tell them one where I die at the end.
Kids eh?
Maddie, UK

Dishonesty and Deviousness:-

It doesn't take long for Children to start telling stories, they love it when you play along, especially when they think you believe them! They can be quite devious at times too, always pushing boundaries!

My Son really loves 'Thomas the Tank Engine' and 'Percy' is his favourite character. This last week he has been blaming Percy for pooing. Whenever I get a whiff of a dirty nappy, I ask if he's pooed and he always says "No." I give him a minute, then he usually comes back and says "Mummy, Percy pooed."
I ask "Did *Percy* poo in *your* nappy?"
He says "Yes" and goes to get the nappy box. That poor steam engine gets the blame for all sorts in our house! Ha Ha!
Lisa, UK

When I was little I remember being outside in the garden and my Mum saw me looking at a spider. She asked me to be careful with it as it was very small and I was much

bigger and could hurt it. I told her I would. My Mum came back when I started crying and saw the spider, dead, in front of me. She asked me if I had done it and I said, matter-of-factly "No Mummy, it put its leg on itself and died."
Sharon, UK

I was having lunch with my six year old Son and we were eating 'Spongebob' pasta. He burped and I said "Don't burp at the table like that!"
He said "I didn't burp, the Spongebob in my mouth farted."
Boys will be boys I guess!
Hannah, USA

The other night my Son wanted to watch a movie. I told him he should let his Sister watch one of *her* movies first so I could make dinner (and she would let me). He was quiet for a while, then said, "Mom I don't want 'The Incredibles' any more. I think I'll give it to her." (Pointing at his Sister)
I said "Really, you don't want that movie? You love that movie!"
He said "Yeah, but I'll share and give it to my Sister."
I said, "That's really sweet of you honey."
Then he looked at me and said "So can we watch 'The Incredibles?' It's one of *her* movies" I just about died laughing!
Mya, USA

One day I had my two youngest girls at the grocery store. The youngest (just under three) pocketed a pack of gum. I saw her do it and gave her a big lecture and made her tell the cashier what she had done. She cried from embarrassment all the way to the car. The oldest girl (just under four) whispered to her sister "Don't cry Sissy, I have gum in my panties!" Back to the grocery store we marched!
Crystal, USA

One time my Cousin informed me that my four year old Niece was doing something she wasn't supposed to do (I don't remember what it was). When I asked her if she was doing something she shouldn't be doing she responded "No. My nose is growing!"
She knew she was lying! Ha Ha!
Mia, USA

Laugh Out Loud! Kids

One day I had my two youngest girls at the grocery store. The youngest (just under three) possessed a pack of gum. I saw her do it and have been big in fits and made her walk the aisles with me, had done. She then took great embarrassment in the way back to... the check out and... at the front of the store. She looked at me and she sighed. But I'm pretending back to his arms each store we watched.

Crystal T.

...
... the way...
... she was... ... that was an aisle and... never... told...
...knowing she... stuff...
...to say no to growing.

Kids' Comments on A New Baby On The Way (Taken From My First Book Laugh Out Loud Pregnancy!):-

I couldn't leave this section out although it has already been included in one of my other books, these stories are just too funny to be left out! I apologise if you have read them before but I'm sure they will make you laugh again!

Why do kids have to be so honest?
The way our little ones grasp the idea of pregnancy can be hilarious, they seem to understand the idea of a baby being inside your belly, but not how it got there or how it comes out (although they will tell you how they think it happens). Some of the funniest stories I've read so far have been about what Children have said or done around us pregnant ladies:-

When I had my 4D scan the other day I was lying there happily watching my boy and my Daughter turned to me and said, "Look Mummy, he's going to be fat like you!"
Charming!
Leah, UK

We found out we were having a boy. My Son said to me, "but Mommy I wanted a Sister!" So I said "Well we can't decide what baby is, the baby decides if it wants to be a girl or boy, and this baby wanted to be a boy". He then said "Okay Mommy, but we need to make another baby in your tummy and I'll tell it to be a girl baby, because I want a Sister."
Lori, USA

I am a teacher and got a surprise last week when speaking to one of the little boys:-
Little Boy: "Is there a baby in your tummy?" *puts his ear to my tummy*
Me: "Erm, maybe, check my bump next week if it is bigger there may be a baby in there."
Little Boy: "Your bump isn't that big."
Me: "Maybe the baby is still small."
Little Boy: "Babies grow in bumps right?"
Me: "Right"
Little Boy: "Do you have two growing up here?" *grabs my boobs*
Me: "No, babies don't grow in there and you can't really touch other people there."
This child is aged five and it was all totally innocent! I nearly fell over laughing.
Maddie, UK

My little boy is always coming out with random funny things! Here's a few:-
I'd just had my scan for my Daughter so was showing him

the pictures and telling him about the baby:-
Me: "look, this is the baby in Mummy's tummy, you're going to be a big Brother" *shows him scan picture*
My Son: "How did that get in there? Did you eat it?"
Me and my Husband just burst out laughing and couldn't stop laughing for ages after that!
Also, I was at my friend's house the other day and her little boy, who is three was messing around and I said "You can't jump about on the sofa, there's a baby in my tummy and you might knock it." He lifted up my top to have a look (and a stroke!) and said "There's a baby in there? How do you get it out?" I called his Mum to explain that one!
Ella, UK

A six year old girl I babysit for was watching my tummy for a while and then looked at me and tactfully said "You look like you're going to have a baby!"
I'm very glad I actually am or I would have been mortified! She then went on to casually say "I think you'll scream when they take your skin off because they have to you know, to get the baby out. Then they put it back on again. You might die."
I kind of went "Erm, no I think I'll be fine. Talk to your Mother about having babies tomorrow!"
It was so awkward, because I hadn't told her about the baby before this, I was waiting for her Mum to approach it with her!
Karla, UK

My eight year old Niece said to my five year old Nephew when she found out I was pregnant "You have to be very

careful to not jump on Auntie's stomach as she is pregnant and you might rupture her womb." I couldn't stop laughing. She has had a very broad vocabulary since she was two!
Lauren, UK

I asked my four year old Niece the other day if she thought the baby would be a boy or a girl, and she said "A girl, because *you're* a girl!" Then looked at me as if this was the most obvious thing in the world, and I was a bit stupid Ha Ha!
Tracey, UK

My Nephews think the baby is in my belly button because it pokes out. They always talk into it and when I ask them why they say "So baby can hear us."
I said "No, baby is not in the belly button."
Sally, UK

Today I was asked by my three year old Cousin "When the baby comes out, can I dress it for you?" which I thought was adorable. Meanwhile my other two little Cousins (seven and six) were putting their hands on my bump and asking "When will the baby kick?" and "Is it sleeping?" and all of a sudden the seven year old says to the six year old "The baby is hiding because you're really loud! You've got to talk like this, (whispers) "Hi little baby, it's your Cousin, I love you!" It was so cute!
Cheryl, UK

My three year old Cousin always asks me where the baby is and why I left her at home! I try to explain that she is still in my tummy but he doesn't seem to get it!
Caroline, UK

My five year old Brother asked me if the baby in my tummy would grow into pineapples! I Don't know where he got that from but I did have to laugh!
Julie, UK

My kids have said some sweet and funny things to me since finding out we're going to have another baby. They are 7, 6, and 4.
6 year old: "Mommy, will they have to cut you open to get the baby out?"
Me: "No honey, probably not."
6 year old: "Will they tell you to push?"
Me: (with a smirk on my face) "Yes honey, they will."
6 year old: "Oh! (Spreads her legs) The baby will come out here (points to vagina), right?"
Me: (on the verge of giggles) "Yes honey, that's right."
4 year old: "Mommy does the baby like pop? Gum? Chicken? Potatoes? Salad?" (It goes on...   Anything I put in my mouth, I am questioned as to whether or not the baby likes it). These questions are because the kids wanted McDonalds one time and I said that the baby doesn't like McDonalds (it has made me sick ever since I've been pregnant).
7 year old: "Mommy, I know a lot about babies. Did you know the umbilical cord is attached to you?"
Me: "Yes I knew that buddy. Do you know what it's for?"
7 year old: "It feeds the baby cos it can't eat real food

yet, right?"
Me: "Yeah, kinda!"
The funniest thing ever was when my kids had a chance to watch a couple of my Mom's cat's kittens being born, and then the seven year old asked me the next day if the baby

will come out of my butt, like the cat!
Helen, USA

My Daughter recently found out I am pregnant with another baby. She later that morning asked me if the baby would be coming out of my tummy (she knows I had a c section with her) or my "big fat bum." Charming!
Chelsea, UK

My four year old Niece said the funniest, cutest thing when I saw her this weekend. Her Mum told her that there was a baby growing in my tummy. Then, when she spoke to my Sister on the phone later she said "Auntie Helen's got a fat tummy, but it's okay because there's a baby growing in it. I'm going to be Cousined!" Then every time anyone spoke too loudly she'd say "Shush, you'll scare the baby." It was so sweet!
Tina, UK

My Son lay down across my lap, facing my belly the other day. He started patting it and said "I love dat baby. I'm gonna look after dat baby." Melt!
Georgina, UK

My Son insists on reading my bump a bed-time story, which I think is very cute. Then he gives it a kiss goodnight and a rub, then gives me a hug and a kiss and tells me "Everything will be fine."
Janine, UK

I had a private scan at sixteen weeks with my Daughter and had a little DVD of her squiggling around. When I showed my Nephew (who is three) I said "Oh look, there is the head, the arms and the legs."
He pointed at the screen and said "And its tail!"
I had to look twice!
Tara, UK

I was at my Sister's the other day and My Nephew was there. The conversation between us went like this:-
Nephew to my Sister: "Are you having another baby Mummy because your tummy is super fat."
Nephew to me: "Shall we play Doctors and Nurses? You be Nurse."
Me: "Ok Doctor, who is here today and what's the problem?"
Nephew: "My Mummy is having a baby and needs to get it out, can you pass me a knife please so I can cut it out?"
My Sister: "OMG you're not delivering my baby like that!"
Stacey, UK

We didn't know how to tell our five year old Niece that we were expecting a baby. We didn't want her to ask where children came from or how it happened, so we sat her down and told her that we were going to have

another baby. She looked at me and then at my Husband, and said "Another one?" We both nodded and then she looked at me and said "It was from him biting you huh?" I just cracked up. Funniest thing I have heard in a while!
Shannon, USA

With my last pregnancy my Mom asked my three year old Son if he wanted a baby Brother or a baby Sister.
His reply was: "I want a train!" Ha Ha!
Wendy, USA

I told my little boy that I was going to have another baby and it took him a while to grasp it, then I said "I'm going to get big and fat like this (put my arms out in front of me to show a bump).
He got teary eyed and said "Oh no you can't, you will pop!"
Becky, UK

My friend's conversation with her three year old today:-
Her: "The baby's kicking."
Him: (laughing) "He's kidding? That's kinda funny!"
Her: "No, not kidding, kicking."
Him: (with a very serious look on his face, gets super close to my tummy and says) "Hey! We is not allowed to kick Mama! You goin' be in trouble!"
Joy, USA

When we told the boys I was pregnant and that 'Mumma' had a baby in her tummy the four year old said "Mumma when dat baby come out?"
I said "not for long time, it has to grow first."
He turns to me and said "Are you sure it's not coz baby shy and doesn't want to play with me?"
Kelly, Lakeland, USA

When my Sister was pregnant last year and told my Sons, my eldest who was about three and a half told everyone his Auntie had eaten a baby!, he looked in her mouth then said "Auntie you shouldn't eat babies!"
Bethany, UK

When we found out I was pregnant again my oldest boy wanted a Sister. I told him I couldn't guarantee it was a girl, it could be another boy. His reply was "If you have another boy can we sell him on ebay, and buy a bike instead?" Ha Ha!
Ruth, UK

This morning, I was crouched over the toilet being sick and a little face pops around the door (my four and a half year old). He said "Mummy, I do love you, even when you are being sick, but can you please try not to sick my baby up?" You've got to love kids for making you stay positive!
Katie, UK

Our Daughter told us that babies come out through the 'magic zip' which appears on your tummy, you zip it open

to get the baby out and then it disappears after the baby has come out! If only it were that simple!
Keeley, UK

Conversation with my four year old Nephew last month:-
Him: "Auntie, when you have a cup of tea does it burn Cousin Charlie's head?"
Me: "No spud."
Him: "What about when you have a shower?"
Me: "Nope, he's got lots of protection."
Him: "Oh okay. Well what time is he coming out?"
Me: "August."
Him: "Is that my birthday?"
Me: "No, your birthday is in January."
Him: "Well in August we'll play football. I'll teach him."
Megan, UK

My Brother's Girlfriend's Daughter is three. One day I switched my Doppler on in an attempt to stop her running riot around my Mum's house. She picked up the Doppler speaker and started talking into it thinking the baby would hear her. Funnily enough, the baby didn't respond (much to her disappointment!). Our conversation went like this:-
Her: "Why is your baby ignoring me?"
Me: "It's not quite big enough to speak yet."
Her: "Or maybe it's just sleeping?"
Me: "He or she might be, but I still don't think he or she is old enough to talk!"
Her: "He or she? Well, if it's a boy I'm throwing him in the bin!"
Nicola, UK

The other day my Boyfriend's Son, who is five, was sitting next to me and decided to lift up my top so he could speak to my baby through my belly button. He said "Hello baby, would you like to share my sandwich? It's ham!"
Vicky, Telford, UK

A little boy asked if I was fat at playgroup yesterday. When told him "No, I'm pregnant" he replied "Oh congratulations! You can never tell." I nearly wet myself he was only about six!
Marie, UK

The other day after playgroup it was raining so we were rushing to get to the cafe to use up the half hour before our bus. My little boy said "I've got fast legs, like Daddy, but you have got your slow legs on because the baby's getting bigger, but it's okay, when the baby comes you can have your fast legs back!" Ha Ha!
Lesley, UK

My Son is six, he was trying to look through my belly button the other day and when I asked him what he was doing he said he was looking for the baby!
Jess, UK

Once the kids were feeling bubs kicking when one told me quite seriously that "You have to put the baby in time out

because you're not allowed to kick!"
Libby, UK

My friend's little girl said to me the other day "If you spin round and round will your baby get dizzy?" Ha Ha! I laughed but I thought it was quite a good question!
Susie, UK

When we were waiting to find out the sex of the baby, my five year old who really has his heart set on a baby Brother kept saying "If it's a girl you will have to take it back to the hospital and exchange it." Ha Ha!
Luckily, we are having another boy so we won't be exchanging!
Donna, UK

I work in a nursery and some of the comments are adorable. Here are some examples:-
Little boy: "When will your baby hatch?"
Little girl: (with massive freaked out eyes as she said it) "The baby is gonna get bigger and bigger and bigger until your head has to fall off, then your baby's head will come out."
Little boy: "I can hear your baby crying!"
Little twin girls: "Is your baby kicking?" If I say no they'll reply "Well mine is!"
Melanie, UK

Two weeks ago I was getting my three year old Son ready to go to the Ante-natal Clinic and he said "Mummy where are we going today?"
So I replied "to Ante-natal."
With a confused look on his little face he asked me "Mummy what does she look like? I haven't met her before, have I?"
Toni, UK

When I was pregnant with my Son, we got my Daughter who was two, one of the baby dolls that cries and wets like a real baby to get her used to the noise. She used the baby's bottle to 'feed' my tummy. She also used to push her mouth on my tummy and yell "Hi Brudder!" just to get him to kick her.
Jacqui, UK

When I was pregnant I came home from hospital after being kept in for a day, and my Son turned to me and said "Erm, Mummy, have they put the baby back in your tummy now?" He had been told that I would go into hospital and that's when the baby would come out so he assumed when I stayed for a day they had taken her out and then put her back in!
Laurie, UK

My Daughter (three years old) crawled into my bed the other morning and started rubbing my belly, then she said "Mommy can the baby come out today?"

When I said "No, she has to keep growing" my Daughter said "But if she grows bigger she'll break your belly!" It was so sweet, she seemed genuinely worried.
Krystal, USA

My 5 year old Daughter asked me the other day "Mommy, Why are you fat?" I said "Because your baby Brother is in my tummy."
To which she replied "But why's your butt fat? The baby can't be in your butt too!"

Thanks Hun!
Whitney, USA

I'm coming up to nine weeks pregnant and we (being my Parents and I) felt it was time to inform my younger Brothers (ages ten and eight) of what was going on.
So, we sat them down, and my Mom told them, "Well, you two are going to be Uncles." Of course, neither one of them understood, so she said, "Your Sister is having a baby."
The older of the two smiled and laughed, normal reaction. But, the youngest one had this terrified look on his face. My Mother asked him what was wrong, to which he replied, "I don't know how to be an Uncle! Can't he (the oldest) just be the Uncle?" We laughed and told him he didn't need to *do* anything to be an uncle, and then he said, "Yeah I do! I need to grow a moustache!"
So, now my eight year old Brother is working on growing his moustache, because that's what makes someone an Uncle. Ha Ha!
Mia, USA

My youngest Brother seems to think I'm just going to "Get really fat and then explode a baby out." Which, from what I understand, he's not far off!
Melanie, UK

My Little girl was on the bus with me one day and was looking at a pregnant lady sat near us. She said "Mummy, why's that lady so fat?"
So I said "She has a baby in her tummy" to which she replied, "Mummy why she eat a baby?" It got most of the other Women on the bus laughing as my Daughter was not exactly quiet when she said it!
Kimberley, UK

My three year old has been shouting through my bellybutton "You can come out now we have put your cot up! Oh and I'm your big Sister!"
Lucy, UK

My Sister is due Christmas Day and she asked her three year old whether he is looking forward to the baby being here. He said "No" so my Sister asked "What are we going to do then when the baby is born?" He said "We will put it back!" Ha Ha!
Jess, UK

Conversation with my three year old Nephew:-

Me: "Look the baby is kicking Mummy's belly!"
Him: *looks at her belly and notices it moving* He gets up and wanders off into his bedroom.
Me: "Where you going?"
Him: *wanders back in with a toy hammer* "Hey baby! If you don't stop hitting my Mummy's belly I'm going to bash you big time!"
Chrissy, UK

When I put my Daughter to bed last night (she's three) she was talking about the baby and I asked her "Are you excited? It won't be long before he is here."
Then she went on to tell me "The baby will be born out of your mouth."
I was like "Erm no, the baby will come out of Mummy's belly" but she told me that no, she was certain the baby was going to come out of my mouth!
Lacey, UK

My Son makes me laugh every day, but today was one of those classics. I've been getting quite a lot of nosebleeds, normal pregnancy stuff. Today while I was getting him dressed, blood started to trickle down my nose a little and he asked "Mummy, why is your nose hurting you?" I wiped it and said "Don't worry, it's just all part of having your little baby Sister."
He stopped for a minute and then he asked "Will she be coming out of your nose?"
Lorna, UK

My Sister has twin boys, aged four and she is pregnant with another baby at the moment. She is due any time soon and so I asked them if they were excited they said "No" and I said "Well how is Mummy then?" They both replied at the same time "Really fat, can't even get your arms round her!" Then to make it even funnier they both held out their arms to show how big her belly was! Ha Ha!
Sarah, UK

My baby Sister was four during the time I was pregnant. She was always so worried about the baby because she is actually more like my Daughter than my Sister. I was eating a banana one day and I was really hungry so I was eating it really fast. Well my little Sister came up to me and said "Sis, slow down! The baby can't chew that big of bites she's gonna choke on it!" then rubbed my belly and said "That's ok baby I got after Mommy for you, you'll be ok!"
Marsha, USA

My four year old was the first to tell me I was pregnant, the one who insisted it was a girl (he was right) and now he wants to hug my tummy, and kiss 'the baby' all the time. He will crawl up on the couch and ask if he can lay his head on my belly. Once he did this and as soon as there was pressure, the baby kicked. He jumped back to ask what happened. I told him the baby kicked him, I was still laughing. He stared at me for a second, then back at my belly. He said "You shouldn't let the baby wear shoes in there." I love it!
Kirsty, USA

Laugh Out Loud! Kids

When I was pregnant with my Son, I was almost seven months gone and I was really into sushi (cooked rolls). We were at my favorite sushi place and we had just eaten dinner when a little girl came up to me. She stared at me for the longest time and then asked "Are you really full?" I tried so hard not to bust out laughing. I just smiled and said "Yes I am!"
Samantha, USA

I was standing in line at a grocery store and there was a Woman with a little boy standing behind me. She was pointing to my stomach and saying to her Son "Look there's a baby in there." He looked at me and then back at her in disbelief, then he pointed to my stomach and shouted "Baby!" His Mother said "Yes there's a baby in there." Then he walked over to a heavy set Man who was standing in front of me in line and he pointed at the Man's stomach and said "Baby?" It was hilarious! The Man in front of me took it very well, he just laughed.
Laura, USA

One day, I was with my family, and we were all talking about how the pregnancy was going. My two year old little Cousin looked at me and went "Where's the baby?" I told him it was in my tummy still. So he lifted up my shirt, in front of everyone, to look at my belly. He then told me that he didn't see it.
I said "Well, you can't see it yet because it's still inside my tummy."
His reply: "Make it come out then."
Jane, USA

I went to the Doctor for the first time last week. My five year old happened to be off school because she had to go to the Doctor for an ear infection. I had to take her with me to the Obstetrician. So I told her they were going to check my tummy to make sure the baby was doing okay. We got into the room and my Doctor decided we should just do a pap (vaginal scan) to get it out of the way since I was seven weeks at the time.

My Daughter was sitting in the chair beside me and they draped the cover over my knees. As they are starting to do the pap she looked at me with his horrible disgusted face and said "Mommy, eww this is gross! What are they doing?" Of course the Doctor and Nurse are laughing and I said "Honey, I told you they had to check Mommy's tummy" so she replied "Well I thought they were going to check from the *other* end!" It was so funny, everyone in the room was laughing hysterically!

Josie, USA

My Mom told me about when she was pregnant with my little Sister. We were out shopping and my Mom was in a dress. All of a sudden, I walked up to a stranger, lifted my Mom's skirt up over her tummy to show off "my baby". My Mom says that she was lucky she was wearing underwear that day, I'm just thinking I'm glad I don't remember!

Cherie, USA

During my last pregnancy I was driving my kindergartener to school and I had to pull over to throw up (morning sickness, yay!) I didn't want her to worry so when I got

back in the truck I told her "It's ok sweetie. Sometimes when Mommies have babies in their tummies they feel a little sick."
The next day I went into her classroom to help out with reading time and her Teacher pulled me aside and surprised me by congratulating me on my new pregnancy and telling me that my Daughter had walked into the classroom and loudly announced that I had puked all over the street and that "Mommy wouldn't get so sick if she'd stop eating all those babies." Ha Ha!
Julie, USA

I showed my six year old Son the DVD from my ultrasound and was pointing out the body parts of the baby. At one point he said "Wait! You mean the baby doesn't have any clothes on?" It cracked me up.
Mary, UK

My two and a half year old Son came up to me one morning and said "Momma look, baby tister in there eating her breakfast!" While pointing at my tummy. It was really sweet, his imagination is unreal.
Jacqui, USA

I am a part-time Nanny for a six year old girl and a couple weeks ago I was taking care of her, and since I hadn't had time to change after my baby shower I was wearing this cute little dress, which happened to show cleavage. So when I bent down to start painting with her, she said "Oh my gosh Summer, your boobies are so full of milk they're about to fall out!" She was so serious, and even though I

tried to explain that since the baby isn't born yet, there's no milk, she kept insisting all night that there was!
Summer, USA

I had been trying to find a way to tell my three year old Son that I'm pregnant. I had a Sister in Law who was nearing the end of her pregnancy so I kept showing him her belly saying, "There's a baby in there." Well he wouldn't believe me and then one day I asked him "Where's the baby?" He walked up to my boobs and said matter of fact, "There mommy, in boob." Ever since he has proceeded to tell everyone that babies come from boobs. Even to the point where one day my Husband was scratching his chest and my Son walked up to him and said, "Oh it's the baby huh?"
Shania, USA

Right now I'm twenty eight weeks pregnant with my second baby. My Son is six years old and he's beyond excited to get a baby Sister. So, he loves rubbing and kissing my belly and saying "Hi" to his Sister all the time, so, he gets that she's in there somewhere. However, we were sitting in bed the other night watching some TV before it was bedtime and a diet pill commercial comes on. He focuses in on it and once it was over he turned to me and said, "Mommy, you need to get some of those to deal with the extra weight and squishiness you've been going through." My Husband almost had a hernia and was doing his best to not laugh out loud. I guess my Son doesn't understand that Mommy has to put on some weight in order to have a healthy baby. So of course, my

dear Husband decided to tell our Son that it would only get worse before it got better! Like Father like Son!
Cindy, USA

I have two younger brothers, and when my Mom was pregnant with the younger one, the older one was about six or seven. Anyway, Mom would always ask us to talk to the baby and he would always say "No." Now, this kid had a knack for deciding how things happened on his own. For instance, when Mom told him she was going to have a baby he asked when she and Dad would be getting married again (because he had figured that babies came from marriage). So one day Mom asked him to talk to the baby and he said, "Okay" and heaved a big sigh, he then proceeded to climb onto the couch, plug my Mother's nose and tilt her head back, opening her mouth. Then he spoke into her mouth because he figured that was the way to talk to the baby!
Jess, USA

I was nine weeks pregnant and had just recently told my two and a half year old Daughter. I walked into her room a couple of days later to clean it and she just lost it. She started crying because she thought the baby was going to take her toys and watch her TV. I explained to her that the baby wasn't big enough to do that yet but when the baby was big enough she should share anyway.
Normally when she wakes up she comes into my room and wakes me up. Well yesterday morning I felt something pushing against my mouth and something digging into my belly button. I opened my eyes and jumped up. My Daughter had a toy in each hand and was

trying to shove them in my mouth and bellybutton. I asked "what are you doing?" She replied, "Well you said share, so I'm letting the baby play with my toys, so eat it!"
Marsha, USA

Every morning during the early stages of pregnancy I would wake up and have to go to the bathroom and be sick, and pee and whatever else. My two year old Daughter would always be sleeping and didn't know that I was being sick. One morning I got up and I didn't hear her get out of bed behind me. I went into the bathroom and just waited for it all to come, as usual. I started throwing up and she came up beside me and started rubbing my back and saying "It's okay Mama, I'll take care of you." Another morning she decided that she wanted to try and get breakfast for herself while I was in the bathroom. I walked into the kitchen and there was milk and cereal everywhere! But somehow she had managed to get two bowls full of milk and cereal as well. She was sitting on the floor eating her cereal and looked at me and said "Mama, I got us breakfast." She patted the floor and says, "Sit down, eat!"
Marie, USA

My Daughter is almost potty trained, and she and my Partner were tickling each other and they decided to gang up on me and start tickling me. Well I was laughing so hard that I couldn't talk and I tried to get up because I really had to pee. I didn't quite make it and ended up slightly peeing myself. My Daughter looked at me and said, "Mommy, do you want to wear one of my pull-ups

so you don't have another accident?" My partner and I cracked up laughing!
Jamie, USA

I used to babysit these two kids, and I ran into them at Wal-mart and was telling their Mom I was pregnant, and the little boy who was four looked up at me and said "Where is the baby?" I put his hand on my tummy and my baby kicked and he said "Oh my God! You ate her! Mommy, Mommy help the baby she can't get out! I always knew you were crazy!" I laughed and we had to explain to him that babies grew inside their Mommy's tummy before they are born. It was hilarious, everybody at Wal-mart was peeking around corners of the aisles trying to figure out what was up!
Alison, New Jersey, USA

My Son is five years old, and he is starting to understand that Mommy has a baby in her belly. So we haven't had 'the birds and the bees' conversation yet and he asked me one night if I knew where babies came from, and I said "Yes, do you?"
He said "Yep, you have to drive to this baby factory that is very far away, then you look at the pictures of all the babies and decide which one you like best. then you got to have surgery cause they got to put the baby inside you, then you come home and wait for it to grow and then a long, long, long time goes by and you got to go to the hospital and they open your belly and take it back out and you get to take it home and play with it." I still don't know who told him this or whether he just tried to work it out for himself!
Lexie, USA

I was sitting down on the couch one evening with my twenty year old Brother and my four year old Son. My Son and I were having a conversation about how babies grow inside ladies bellies, and I said to my Son "You know you were once a little baby inside Mama's tummy." My Son replied with "Yeah then I grew bigger and bigger and I came out your mouth." My Brother and I just looked at each other and burst out laughing, it was so funny. The next day we had to go to the Doctor's surgery for a check-up as I was pregnant again and my Son knows that I have another baby in my tummy. While we were sitting in the waiting room this Man walks in with a rather large beer belly and my son piped up with "Mama that Man has a baby in his belly too, just like you but his baby is bigger than your one." Oh my face turned bright red! Needless to say I had to share it with my Brother as soon as I finished my appointment and he thought it was hilarious too!
Stephanie, USA

I have a two year old Nephew and one day I asked him what my Son's name was going to be because I love the way he says the name I picked but he replied with "His name is Bob, well his real name is not Bob but I'm gonna call him Bob cause you don't always have to call someone their name, like you call me Bubba so I'm calling him Bob and don't try to tell me not to." Ha Ha!
Natasha, UK

At our twelve week ultrasound we took our eight year old Son along to meet his Brother or Sister who's living in my tummy. While staring at the monitor, seeing this weird-looking object twisting and twirling while Mommy and Daddy are going on about how big the baby has grown, out of the blue he said "I'm having a Sister." Mystified we asked him how he knew since it was too early to tell from the ultrasound and what would an eight year old boy know about such things? Without blinking he replied: "She does not have a penis. Look! There's nothing between her legs!" I almost died as the Doctor couldn't look up, he was laughing too much. I explained that we wouldn't be able to see a penis just yet as the baby was too small!
Kerry, UK

I was sitting in the back seat of the car with my three year old Daughter, talking to her about how she's going to be a big Sister. I decided to ask her if she would like to go shopping with me for a toy for the baby. She said "Yeah I'm going to get the baby a toy but I have to wait till the baby comes out."
I said "Why do you have to wait?"
She said "The box won't fit in your belly so I have to wait."
So funny!
Cheryl, UK

Kids' Comments on New Baby When Here (Taken From My Second Book Laugh Out Loud Babies!):-

If you read my previous book then you will have read all the hilarious comments from siblings about their little Brother or Sister to be, but when the baby actually arrives, the situation changes and makes way for even more funny comments:-

We had to take our six month old to an emergency appointment at the Hospital recently and on our travels our three year old asked if we're going to collect a new baby. Then when I reminded him his new baby Brother is already here he casually asked "Can we not swap him?" Of course I said No!
Frankie, UK

My three year old Nephew says some cute things. When his little Brother was born I was watching both of them and the baby started to cry so my Nephew said "Well he's probably just hungry."

I said "Yeah you're right, but he'll be ok until Mommy gets back, she'll be here in a couple of minutes."
He said "Oh no, it's ok, you've got boobs so you can feed him." I just about died laughing, then told him that only Mommies can feed their baby!
Sarah, USA

My five year old Son knows babies have milk from Mummy's boobies but he cracked me up the other day when he asked "Where are the straws for the baby to get the milk out of?"
Erin, UK

When my Son was born, I breastfed him. On one of the mornings that I got to lay in bed and feed him my Daughter came into the room, cocked her head sideways and said, "Mommy, why brudder eat you boob?" After I had explained, she 'breastfed' all her baby dolls!
Sherri, South Dakota, USA

When my Son was a few months old my Mum was round visiting and I nipped to the shops. He started getting hungry just before I got home so Mum was comforting him (as he was breastfed). My eldest Daughter who was three at the time said, "Grandma, you've got boobies, why don't you just feed him?" I had to explain that one when I got home!
Anna, UK

My Nephew was watching his Mom breastfeeding his new baby Sister. After watching for a while and looking very confused, he asked: "Mom why have you got two? Is one for hot milk and one for cold milk?"
Me and my Sister couldn't stop laughing!
Donna, UK

I was breastfeeding my Daughter when she about five days old and my four year old Son wanted me to play. I said "I can't, I'm feeding the baby." So he went to the fridge and got our milk out and said "Here Mummy, just give her some of this." I didn't find it funny at the time, but everyone else did!
Belinda, UK

I remember when I brought my second Daughter home from the Hospital, my eldest Daughter was just over two and a half. I was holding the baby, and she said, "You always hold that baby, put it down!"
When I explained to her that Mummy had to hold the baby to feed her she looked at me and said (very seriously) "Well I think it's time for that baby to go back then."
On another occasion she was asked by a friend of mine how she liked having a baby Sister, to which she replied "Not much, all she does is cry!" Ha Ha!
Gloria, UK

I was at Kindergarten with my nearly four year old Daughter and my eight month old Son. I was sitting

breastfeeding my Son when another child came up to me and asked "What you doing?"
I replied "I'm feeding my baby."
"Oh" he said and went out to play. After I had finished breastfeeding, my Son enjoyed a can of egg custard. I cleaned him up and popped him into the pushchair. The same Boy from earlier returned and asked "What did you feed your baby?"
I replied, "First milk, then egg custard." He stood, obviously in deep thought, for a few seconds and then asked "Which booby was the egg custard in?" I laughed until I cried!
Jenna, USA

My eldest Daughter is eight years old and one day I was cooking dinner and my three month old started fussing. I asked my eight year old to hold her for me until I finished. She was standing in the kitchen with me holding the baby. She looked at me and said, "Mommy, I wish the baby was a magnet so I could just stick her to the refrigerator." It took me a while to recover after laughing so much!
Alison, USA

When my Son was two I was playing with his Sister who was probably about four weeks old or so. My Son came up to me with a very annoyed look on his face and said, "No, Mama! Amy is *my* Sister. Your Sister is Emma. Go play with her so Amy can play with me."
Annabel, USA

I was in the waiting room at the Doctors and reading my two year old Son 'Hansel and Gretel' and we were chatting about the pictures etc. We got to the page where the scary old Witch is luring them inside. He pointed to her and yelled "Gramma!" I couldn't stop laughing! The people in the Doctor's office thought it was quite humorous too.
Abby, USA

My three year old Daughter was standing outside with my Mom and my neighbor, chatting away. My Daughter was playing happily in the grass when my neighbor's girlfriend asked for a corkscrew to open her wine bottle. I told her that I actually don't drink wine so I don't own a corkscrew. My Daughter promptly spoke up and said "My Gramma gots one cause she's a wino!" Dear me, where do they come up with this stuff? I certainly never said it to her!
Elizabeth, USA

I'm a breastfeeding Mum and feed in front of my toddler. The other day she was feeding her teddy and she shouted at the teddy "No bite!" and sent him to the naughty corner! I suppose I didn't realise how much she was taking in until I saw her copying!
Maddie, UK

My Son saw my Sister breastfeeding my Niece and asked my Sister what she was doing. My Sister calmly said that the baby was eating. My Son got a very concerned look on his face and asked "She's eating you?" He then came to me and said "Mom! baby's eating Auntie under her shirt!"

I said, "What?"
He said, "Baby is eating Auntie!" I then had to explain that babies eat *from* their Mommies, they don't actually eat them, and that my Sister was going to be okay!
Ruby, USA

One night after my youngest was born, we were all out to dinner. I noticed he was getting hungry so I handed him to my Mom so I could run to the ladies room. He started crying and my eldest asked "What's wrong?" Mom told him that the baby was hungry, so he lifted my Mom's shirt while saying "'So feed him, you have big boobies!" She told him that her 'boobies' didn't have milk in them. He ran to the bathroom and told me "Your Mother is rude and hates the baby! She refuses to share her boobs!" We tried to explain but he didn't get it. Poor guy was upset with her for over a month and kept saying how rude she was! Ha Ha!
Jennifer, USA

A few weeks had passed since I had my Daughter and I was outside the School gates, dropping my five year old Son off, and in front of all the other Mums he asked (very loudly) "Mummy, do those ladies all have jelly
bellies because they've had babies?" I wanted the floor to swallow me up!
Kirsty, UK

I was out shopping with my four year old Daughter while my Husband was home with my baby boy. We had finished and were stood in quite a long queue at the

checkout, when my Daughter started chatting to an old Man behind us. She casually told him (and the rest of the shop) that her baby Brother was at home with Daddy. I thought this was quite sweet until she continued by saying "He came out of my Mummy's vagina. It had to stretch really big" (she outstretched her arms to show how big). I was mortified, especially when I saw the look of shock on the old Man's face. My Daughter finished by saying (with a big grin on her face) "It's ok though, because it stretched back again." The old Man just nodded and I could hear the stifled giggles from the other people who had overheard. I turned a shade of red I don't think I've been before!
Nadia, UK

My Son told me he was playing 'Mummies and Daddies' at School when the baby started crying. The Mummy said "Oh no, why is the baby crying?" My Son said "It just wants boobies." He has a baby Sister and is used to the baby crying! Ha Ha!
Caroline, UK

When my Son was about 3 weeks old, my Daughter had been ever so excited about helping Mummy feed the baby before he arrived and didn't really understand when I said "Only Mummy can feed him at first because he has 'booby milk' but when he has bottles you can help." When she questioned why she couldn't yet I explained she didn't have boobies yet as she was too little. Anyway, the baby was due for a feed one day and got to crying stage on my Husband's chest before I got to him. I nearly wet myself when my Daughter said very seriously "Don't

cry baby, Daddy will give you some milk from his boobies in a minute and then you won't be hungry." I had to explain that only Mummies boobies give milk. After that my Husband went on a diet to get rid of the 'moobs' ha ha!
Nicola, UK

When I was pregnant with my youngest I asked my Daughter (who was 6) if she wanted a Sister or a Brother. She said "What I want is a monkey." After her little Sister was born and was crying one day, my older Daughter said "See, I told you we should get a monkey."
Maria, USA

That's all for this book, I hope you enjoyed reading! There are two more books in the 'Laugh Out Loud!' series:-

Laugh Out Loud! – Pregnancy
Laugh Out Loud! – Babies

If you are leaving a review, thank you for your feedback! (you can write a review on the Amazon site or on goodreads)

You can find the Laugh Out Loud! Blog at http://laughoutloud-books.blogspot.co.uk/ where I am constantly adding new stories from my own family, especially comments from my little boy who makes me laugh every day!

I have also got a Facebook page dedicated to this series where you can add your own comments and stories at https://www.facebook.com/pages/Laugh-Out-Loud/420362314743645

Happy reading!
Sharon Irish

www.ingramcontent.com/pod-product-compliance
Lightning Source LLC
Chambersburg PA
CBHW071502040426
42444CB00008B/1456